Ng

...ker Papers

Ranginui Walker is from Whakatōhea of Ōpōtiki. He is married to Deirdre and they have three children. He was educated at St Peter's Māori College, Auckland Teachers College and the University of Auckland. He is currently Professor in Māori Studies at the University of Auckland.

In public life Dr Walker was chairman of the Auckland District Māori Council for fifteen years and a member of the New Zealand Māori Council for twenty years. He has written many papers on Māori education, culture and politics and has contributed regular columns to the *New Zealand Listener* and to *Metro* magazine.

NGĀ PEPA A RANGINUI

The Walker Papers

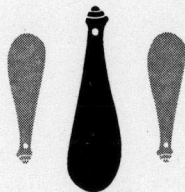

Ranginui Walker

PENGUIN BOOKS

PENGUIN BOOKS
Penguin Books (NZ) Ltd, cnr Airborne and Rosedale Roads, Albany,
Auckland 1310, New Zealand
Penguin Books Ltd, 27 Wrights Lane, London W8 5TZ, England
Penguin Putnam Inc, 375 Hudson Street, New York, NY 10014, United States
Penguin Books Australia Ltd, 487 Maroondah Highway,
Ringwood, Australia 3134
Penguin Books Canada Ltd, 10 Alcorn Avenue, Toronto,
Ontario, Canada M4V 3B2
Penguin Books (South Africa) Pty Ltd, 5 Watkins Street,
Denver Ext 4, 2094, South Africa
Penguin Books India (P) Ltd, 11, Community Centre, Panchsheel Park,
New Delhi 110 017, India

Penguin Books Ltd, Registered Offices: Harmondsworth, Middlesex, England

First published by Penguin Books (NZ) Ltd, 1996

This Print on Demand digital edition created by Penguin Books (NZ) Ltd, 2001

Designed by Richard King
Typeset by Egan-Reid Ltd, Auckland
Digital printing by APG, Maryborough

ISBN 0 14 1006064

Contents

Acknowledgements

I WANT TO THANK Geoff Walker for the idea of publishing a collection of my papers in book form and engaging Graham Adams to edit them. Graham has done an admirable job of bringing together a disparate collection of papers and editing them so that they hang together in a reasonably coherent form. I am also grateful to my colleague Dr Jane McRae who agreed at short notice to enter macrons marking long vowels in Māori words. Above all, I am thankful to my wife Deirdre for her loyal support over all the years and for help with proof-reading the final draft of the manuscript.

Introduction

WHEN I WAS an undergraduate at Auckland University, some of the writing we were given as students was intellectually stimulating. I was particularly turned on by exhortations to read Marx, Huxley and Darwin, the taboo authors of my religious upbringing. Otherwise much of the reading was bland, boring, and in some cases downright incomprehensible. I never did get to understand Talcott Parsons' *Towards a General Theory of Action*. At that time Māori students thought their Pākehā counterparts had some kind of code that gave them an edge at university. But not even my Pākehā mates could give a lucid explanation of Parsons' theory. It was comfortable to know that I was capable of making my own judgement about what constituted good writing and what should be dismissed as opaque obfuscation.

No doubt much of the turgid writing which plagued the life of undergraduates was motivated by the academy's dictum of 'publish or perish'. Because of this academic treadmill, I felt we hapless students were drowning in an ocean of paper. I made a private resolution to myself not to add to the pile of pretentious papers that passed as scholarship. In view of that resolution, the reader deserves an explanation for the title of this book.

I grew up in the small town of Ōpōtiki in the eastern Bay of Plenty where there was an informal social divide between Māori and Pākehā. Māori were the dispossessed underclass, refugees of an illicit military invasion in 1865. Pākehā, the descendents of military settlers, were the beneficiaries of that invasion. They were the landowners. They controlled the judicial apparatus, the borough council, and the commercial life of the town. They also ran the schools, the means by which the minds of the powerless were infected with the grand narrative of the British Empire.

These patently obvious disparities in power relations between Māori and Pākehā were papered over by exhortations to 'forget the past' and to go on to a rosy future as 'one people'. But how could the past be forgotten when my mother Wairata talked about raupatu, the unjust confiscation of Whakatohea lands for the execution of Carl Volkner as a government spy by the Hauhau guerrilla fighter Kereopa Te Rau? Although he was not involved, the Whakatohea chief Mokomoko was apprehended and executed along with Kereopa. To add insult to injury, grants of Whakatohea land were made to Te Arawa 'loyalists', the iwi to which Kereopa belonged.

During my years as a teacher trainee and as a university student, I realised that Ōpōtiki was a microcosm of power relations of Pākehā domination and Māori subordination in the rest of New Zealand. There were no Māori role models in positions of power at teachers college or university. In the Auckland regional office of the Education Department there was not one Māori in sight. Not even in the specialist area of the Māori School Service. The only place that a Māori could be found was in the ghetto of the Department of Māori Affairs. There, war heroes, officers and commanders of the Māori Battalion could be found in the subordinate middle level of the organisation.

The subordinate position of the Māori was reflected in Parliament, where Māori representation had been limited to four seats in a house of 80. The electoral provision of establishing a new seat for every intercensal population increase of 30,000 did not apply to Māori representation. True, there were occasional glimmers of hope, such as the appointment of Sir Charles Bennett, a commander of the Māori Battalion, as High Commissioner to Malaysia. But he was merely the exception that proved the rule of Māori subjection. Despite his success with the tāngata whenua of Malaysia, who recognised him as one of their own by awarding him a knighthood in the face of resistance by our government, the experiment was not repeated.

Imagine the possibilities of the appointment of the late Sir James Henare, also a Māori Battalion commander, to

Saudi Arabia during the oil crisis. But at that time such imagination was too much to hope for in the mandarins of Foreign Affairs. They do not understand the natural affinity that indigenous people of the world, who have experienced the yoke of colonisation, have for each other.

The obvious social and political disparities between Māori and Pākehā were papered over by ideological mystification and deception which descended occasionally to the level of hypocrisy. Under the ideology of 'one people', state mandarins promoted New Zealand as having the finest race relation in the world. At that time Māori were politically quiescent, while in the cauldron of South Africa and in the southern states of America, blacks were rising up against injustice. I knew it would be only a matter of time before the same challenge would be mounted in New Zealand. From my understanding of reality, I wanted to be part of that challenge when it came. To that end I equipped myself with a PhD, so that my view of reality would be accorded the same respect that was given to Pākehā commentators and 'experts' who made pronouncements and wrote authoritative books, dissertations, and reports on Māori failings.

The catalyst for the challenge to Pākehā domination was urbanisation in the post-war years of 1950–70. In that period Māori had to accomplish the two developmental tasks of learning to survive in the capitalist economy, and transplanting their culture into the urban milieu. The successful accomplishment of those tasks was symbolised by the building of urban marae. With their culture secure, Māori leaders turned their attention to the third developmental task of politicisation and the emancipatory struggle against domination.

My appointment as secretary to the Auckland District Māori Council in 1969, and election as chairman in 1974, coincided with the rise of Māori activism. The decade was characterised by the mounting of annual protests at Waitangi, the Māori Land March in 1975, land occupations at Bastion Point and Raglan, the police shooting of Daniel Houpapa, and the trauma of the Stormtrooper confrontation with police at Moerewa in 1979.

During these turbulent years, much of the public discourse in the media lacked insight into Māori behaviour. I was strategically placed as an academic at the interface between the two cultures to counter some of the negative media perceptions of Māori that characterised the period. Consequently, I was constantly engaged in counter hegemonic discourse against power-brokers of the state in the media of radio, newspapers and television.

My writing as a columnist for the *Listener* between 1973–90 enabled me to enter the Māori perceptions of the events of that period into the public record. At that time I preferred to pitch my writing at the general public instead of writing for an academic audience. I felt that some academics spent too much time incestuously arguing over their intellectual chestnuts instead of sharing them with the people to bring about enlightenment and social change. That is where social change begins, in the hearts and minds of ordinary people, who are just as capable as academics of intellectual analysis. None of the Māori activists I knew had read Marx, Gramsci or Friere. But because of domination and subordination they were the most successful practitioners of the academy's emancipatory theories that it was my privilege to know.

As a communicator between the worldviews of Māori and Pākehā, I increasingly found myself being invited to write papers for conferences and chapters in books. Because my colleagues in the academic fraternity sought me out, I responded by writing more papers that I can remember, thus contradicting my earlier resolution not to add to the mounting pile of paper. The end results of this writing are distilled in Ngā Tau Tohetohe, Years of Anger; Ka Whawhai Tonu Mātou, Struggle Without End, and now Ngā Pepa a Ranginui, The Walker Papers.

1: BEING MĀORI

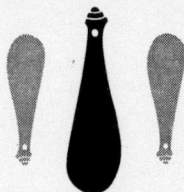

In the beginning

THE WORLD VIEW of the Māori is encapsulated in whakapapa, the description of the phenomenological world in the form of a genealogical recital. Implicit in the meaning of whakapapa are ideas of orderliness, sequence, evolution, and progress. These ideas are embodied in the sequence of myths, traditions and tribal histories. They trace the genesis of human beings from the creation of the universe to the creation of the first woman and, thereafter, the development of culture and human institutions.

Māori philosophers conceptualised the creation of the universe in three epochs. The sequence begins with Te Kore, the vast emptiness of space, followed by Te Pō, the darkness of inner space, which in turn was succeeded by Te Ao Mārama, the world of light, in which humans live.

The first two epochs are timeless. They correspond to aeons of cosmological time, when the seeds of the universe scattered throughout space came together to form earth and sky.[1] The world of light, on the other hand, is characterised by a time-scale measured through human existence.

Although the tohunga, who were the priests and keepers of knowledge in the schools of learning, worked out a lunar calendar, and an annual cycle of seasons, time was not calculated in terms of years, centuries or millennia. In Māori philosophy, there were only two dimensions to time – past and future. The past was designated mua, and the future termed muri. Both had double meanings. Mua also meant 'in front of', or 'ahead'. This means that the past is conceived of as being in front of human consciousness, because only the present and the past are knowable. Muri, designating the future, also means 'behind', because the future cannot be seen. Thus, the individual is conceptualised as travelling backwards in time to the future, with the present unfolding in front as a continuum into the past.

Since the past and the present constitute a single field of unified knowledge, the myths and traditions which elaborate the various layers of whakapapa are both historic and ahistoric. They belong to the historic present because the narratives of mythology and tradition are constantly referred to in public discourse by living exponents of Māori knowledge. The narratives about gods, culture heroes and ancestors are located in time by their position in the sequence on the genealogical table of the whakapapa.

The creation myth

During the first cosmological epoch of Te Kore, the primaeval matter that comprised the seeds of the universe scattered throughout the vast emptiness of space came together to form earth and sky. Although Te Kore was a timeless epoch, it was characterised by divisions, each with its own descriptive terminology. Thus Te Kore, the void, becomes Te Kore Tē Whiwhia, the void in which nothing could be obtained, and Te Kore Tē Rawea, the void in which nothing could be done.[2]

The second epoch, Te Pō, was also a timeless period with its own descriptive divisions. Te Pō is variously described as: Te Pō Nui, the great darkness; Te Pō Roa, the long night; Te Pō Uriuri, the deep dark; Te Pō Kerekere, the intense dark; Te Pō Tangotango, the intensely dark; and Te Pō Te Kitea, the dark in which nothing could been seen.[3]

These descriptions of the nature of Te Pō culminate in a numerical sequence of darkness, which implies a progression rather than a static state. The sequence begins with Te Pō Tuatahi, the first night, proceeding to Te Pō Tuangahuru, the tenth night, to the hundredth unto the thousandth night.[4] This great epoch of darkness is a metaphor for the mind. Without light there was no knowledge. The abyss of dark ignorance prevailed.

There are variations in the number of descriptive terms between different tribal schools of learning for the first two epochs of space and darkness. But no matter how variable the tables are, they all culminate in two names, Ranginui and Papatūānuku. The scholar Te Rangikaheke, of the Rangiwewehi tribe, describes Ranginui the sky father, and Papatūānuku the earth mother, as the first cause.[5] This primaeval pair had generated themselves in space to form earth and sky. They were the cause of darkness because of the close coupling of their bodies in the act of procreation.

During the procreative union of Rangi and Papa, some schools of learning intercalated two additional lists of descriptive terms which convey the idea of the spontaneous generation and evolution of primitive life forms.[6] This evolutionary process culminates in sapient beings capable of reason and therefore seeking enlightenment.

List One		List Two	
Te Pū	the root cause	Te Rapunga	the seeking
Te Weu	the rootlets	Te Kukune	the growth
Te More	the taproot	Te Pupuke	the swelling
Te Aka	the vine	Te Hihiri	the energy
Te Tipuranga	the growth	Te Mahara	the thought
		Te Hinengaro	the mind
		Te Manako	the longing

The reason for the longing and seeking was the dark and cramped conditions which the six sons of Rangi and Papa endured between the bodies of their parents. They longed for light to enter the world so that they and their descendants might flourish.

Tāne Mahuta, the god of forests, proposed the separation of earth and sky. Four of his brothers tried and failed to push their parents apart. Tane succeeded, by pushing upwards with his legs and downwards against the earth with his shoulders. This demonstration of problem solving by lateral thinking is a model built into Māori thought. The event is marked by the name Tāne te toko o te rangi. The name is a metaphor which captures the image of Tāne, as god of the forest, propping up the heavens with his legs. The name, and the myth that generated it, imbues the landscape with meaning. Its veracity is attested to in the experience of those who enter the forest. The mighty kauri and tōtara trees are Tāne's props holding up the sky, which can be discerned through the green canopy overhead.

Tāne's separation of earth and sky ushered in Te Ao Mārama, the third epoch of the world of light. At first, the world was dimly lit. The gods placed the sun in the sky to shine by day, and the moon and stars to shine at night. As the moon waned and disappeared at the end of its monthly cycle, it renewed itself by bathing in the life-giving waters of Tāne the procreator.

The world of light created by Tāne is the domain of human beings. But the gods, whose domain is Te Pō, are the source of all knowledge. They mediate the transition between the metaphysical domain of Te Pō, to the phenomenological world of Te Ao Mārama.

The separation of earth and sky was a pivotal event in the creation. It was characterised by Te Rangikaheke as the first evil.[7] Letting light into the world was the analogue to the biblical story of eating fruit from the tree of knowledge. With that knowledge, good and evil came into the world. The evil that followed was conflict between the gods, but the good that came out of it was the elaboration of the phenomenological world known to human beings.

Tāne's brother Tāwhirimātea disagreed over the separation. That disagreement culminated in the war of the gods, which presaged the wars of men. As god of winds and tempests, Tāwhirimātea attacked the great forests of Tāne, smashing down his trees in revenge for his parents. They became food for grubs, rot and decay.

Having vanquished Tāne, Tāwhirimātea turned his wrath on the oceanic domain of Tangaroa. Tangaroa's descendant was Punga, who in turn produced Ikatere and Tū-te-wehiwehi. These descendants differed over how to escape the wrath of Tāwhirimātea. That difference led to a separation of the species. Ikatere fled and hid in the depths of the ocean, to become the progenitor of fishes. Tū-te-wehiwehi fled inland to become the progenitor of reptiles.[8] The myth indicates that Māori philosophers thought of fish and reptiles as being descended from a common ancestor.

Tāwhirimātea then directed his wrath against the other two brothers who agreed to the separation. But he could not find them. Papatūānuku felt sorry for these junior sons so she hid them in the earth. Only their hair was above ground, so the storm passed harmlessly overhead. But these sons were condemned to a lowly estate. Rongomatāne became the god of kūmara, agriculture and peaceful arts. Haumiatiketike became the god of fernroot and wild plants.

Tāwhirimātea sought out and attacked Tūmatauenga for supporting the separation. Of all the brothers, Tūmatauenga alone stood undefeated by Tāwhirimātea. But he resented the desertion by his elder brothers, and sought to punish them for being cowed by Tāwhirimātea. Tu punished Tāne by snaring the birds of the forest and consuming them. He fashioned nets to harvest the descendants of Tangaroa for food. After that he fashioned spades and baskets out of some of Tāne's trees and plants to dig up the descendants of Rongomatāne and Haumiatiketike for food.[9]

The creation myth personifies Tūmatauenga as the god of war and archetype of the fierce and war-like temperament of man. Tūmatauenga's assertion of dominance over the natural domains of his brothers is the charter for the superordinate position of human beings in the natural order. The subordination and commodification of the descendants of Tāne, Tangaroa, Rongo, and Haumiatiketike transformed them from the sacred estate of gods to the profane level of artifacts and food.

This transformation introduced into the world the fundamental dichotomy between tapu and noa, the sacred and profane. Tapu emanated from Te Pō, the realm of gods. Only the gods could undo the tapu from their own creations and make them available for human use in the world of light.

That task was accomplished by Tūmatauenga, who laid down appropriate incantations for accessing the products of each domain of nature.

These gods were all males. They embodied ira atua, the divine principle. Tāne searched for the female element in nature to create ira tāngata, the human principle, but it was not found. He concluded a separate act of creation was needed. Tāne fashioned the first human named Hine-ahuone, the earth-formed maid, out of Papatūānuku. He breathed his mauri, the life force, into her. Thus, being is a duality of ira atua and ira tāngata in human beings. But humans, unlike gods, are not immortal. When the mauri leaves the body, death ensues. Only the wairua, the spiritual remnant of ira atua, survives death to return to Te Pō from whence it came.

Tāne cohabited with Hineahuone and produced a daughter named Hinetītama, the dawn-maid. He cohabited with her to beget other children. Inevitably, Hinetītama asked Tāne who her father was. He evaded the question by telling her to ask the posts of their house. Hinetītama knew intuitively that her own husband was her father. She fled from Tāne to the portal of the underworld. Tāne pursued Hinetītama but she commanded him not to follow. He was to remain on earth to care for their children in the world of light. She would wait to receive them into the world of night as Hinenuitepō, the goddess of death.[10] Hinetītama's flight from Tāne dramatised the serious nature of incest, thereby setting the social precedent for the incest taboo.

Although the gods created the universe, it is evident from the creation myth that the Māori philosophers concep-tualised the gods in their own image and likeness. Like humans, the primaeval pair Rangi and Papa coupled in darkness to produce offspring. As in human society, the offspring were ranked according to their order of birth. In the quarrel that ensued over the separation of their parents, the gods, like their human counterparts, battled for domination. In a society that based chieftainship on primo-geniture, Tūmatauenga's defeat of his elder brothers indicated that the principle was not incontrovertible.

Bravery, skill and determination in the face of adversity could overcome an inferior rank.

In the personification of Papatūānuku as the earth-mother, some of the primary values of Māori culture are laid down in the creation myth. The food that springs from the bosom of Papatūānuku sustains life. For this reason the earth is loved and cherished as a mother is loved. Since humans were created out of the earth by Tāne, death is conceptualised as a return to the bosom of Papatūānuku. There, at the portal of Rarohenga, the Hades of the Māori, Hinenuitepō awaits as a benevolent mother-figure to receive the dead. Rarohenga was not a place to be feared because it was thought of as another world where the dead would be reunited with their ancestors.

The Māui and Tawhaki myths

The Māui and Tawhaki sequence of myths, which follow the creation, provide legitimating charters for the origins of culture and the elaboration of human institutions and customary practices. In Māori philosophy, gods are the source of knowledge. For this reason, intermediary ancestors between gods and humans fetch knowledge from their ancestors above them in the whakapapa, and transmit it to human descendants who come after them. The demi-god Māui-tikitiki-a-Taranga is one of the myth heroes who fulfilled that mediating role.

Māui was the archetype culture hero who overcame the disadvantage of being the last born of five brothers to gain fame and adulation as a benefactor of humankind. He stands as a model to all tēina (juniors) that they too can succeed provided they have the required personal qualities. The favoured personality traits, as exemplified by Māui, include intelligence, cunning, initiative, boldness and determination.

In his first exploit, Māui deceived his mother and spied on her to discover the country where his father lived. Māui's search for his father dramatised the pivotal nature of the relationship. Finding his father was necessary for the performance of his tohi (purification) rite, and therefore his legitimation in the eyes of the world.

With his place in the world secure, Māui set about acquiring knowledge from his supra-normal ancestors. From his kuia Murirangawhenua, he acquired knowledge concerning the special properties of bone for the manufacture of hooks and weapons. From another grandmother, Mahuika, he wrested the secret of fire. In both cases he used cunning and deceit to achieve his goals. He did so because the relationship between old and young is one of ambivalence.

Kuias are the keepers of knowledge, which the young need to succeed in the world. Kuia do not surrender their knowledge lightly, because its possession is central to their own status and mana. For this reason, the kuia transmitted their knowledge slowly to a carefully selected descendant. Māui had the right qualities to receive the knowledge, but he wanted it immediately because he was eager to take up the task of transforming the world. The end justified tricking his kuia to acquire the knowledge quickly.

Māui used his knowledge to benefit humankind by fishing up the North Island of New Zealand, and slowing the sun's passage across the sky. He also provided human beings with a valuable companion, and a source of food and raw materials for cloaks and bone artifacts, when he turned his brother-in-law Irawaru into a dog.

While the act of transforming his brother-in-law might appear to be a harsh and capricious act against someone who merely bested him at fishing, the event dramatised the uneasy nature of the relationship between brothers-in-law. It is a recurring theme in myth and tradition.

In the course of his adventures, Māui set precedents in social etiquette for introductions to strangers, the use of mākutu (sorcery) against rivals, prayers to the gods for deliverance from danger, and thanksgiving for successful expeditions. But in his quest for the ultimate benefit of immortality for humankind, Māui lost the contest against his ancestor Hinenuitepō.

The flaw in Māui was the error made by his father

Makeatutara in the performance of his tohi ritual. In his assault upon Hinenuitepō, Māui was unable to complete the task of reversing the birth process. When the upper half of his body got stuck, the goddess awoke and crushed Māui with her formidable vaginal dentata. Māui's failure is the Māori rationale for death. Since the greatest culture hero was not able to conquer death, lesser mortals must be reconciled to it as the end of all human beings.

After Māui, his brother Rupe continued the elaboration of customary practices. Rupe's search for his sister Hinauri indicates the primacy of the relationship between siblings in Māori society. His search took him to the heavenly abode of Rehua and back to earth again. The encounter with Rehua in the celestial realm laid down basic cultural norms concerning food, the separation of the sacred and the profane, and proper sanitary arrangements for the disposal of human waste. The derivation of the charters for these practices from the gods ensured compliance in the terrestrial realm.

Rupe eventually found Hinauri living at Motutapu with the high chief Tinirau. When Hinauri's son Tuhuruhuru was born, his purification rite was performed by the high priest Kae. Kae's killing of Tinirau's pet whale, which was loaned to ferry him home, became a *casus belli* between them. As the villain of the drama, Kae deserved to die. But instead of sending a war party after his enemy, Tinirau sent a group of women to beguile Kae's people with their charms. Kae was abducted in the dead of night, delivered to Tinirau and executed. Underlying this event are two of the basic canons of Māori warfare. Firstly, utu is a social duty. Secondly, the element of surprise is fundamental to the strategy of war.

In the vendetta that followed the death of Kae, Whakatau-pōtiki's brother Tūwhakararo was killed by his affines. This incident reaffirmed the dangerous nature of the relationship with in-laws while Whakatau's heroic exploits against his enemies elaborated the canons of leadership in war. They included disguise, spying and reconnaissance to gain intelligence about the enemy, interrogation of prisoners, denial of intelligence to the enemy, lone exploits, and single combat. For the commander of warriors, the rules included careful selection of personnel, military drill, practising order of battle, and the disposition of warriors into assault, supporting, and reserve columns.

The Tawhaki cycle of myths continued the elaboration and reinforcement of Māori culture and customs. The themes include: conflict with brothers-in-law, pursuit of revenge, the naming of a son to commemorate conflict, the filial duty of recovering a father's bones from the enemy, reiteration of the canons of war laid down by Whakatau, establishment of death as the sanction underlying tapu, acquisition of knowledge from a kuia, and the search for a wife. Tawhaki's dangerous ascent to the celestial realm to recover his wife dramatised the primacy of the husband-wife relationship in Māori society. It ranks alongside the bonds between siblings, children, and parents.

In the next generation, Tawhaki's son Wahieroa was killed by the demoniacal Matukutakotako. The death was avenged by his son Rata, who was not intimidated by the power of his adversary. Following the military precedents set by Whakatau and Tawhaki, Rata found the demon's weak point and slew him.

The rules of war, laid down in the realm of mythology by demi-gods and culture heroes, are powerful energy-releasing and motivating forces in human life. They explain the successes of Māori leaders in the historic period against an imperial army that outnumbered and outgunned them. Their war strategies were more subtle than the European traditions of bombardment and the expenditure of human life to take an objective by frontal assault.

The traditions

The mythological charters for Māori customs and social institutions were projections of current social practice back in ancestral time to the Hawaiki homeland, the Māori equivalent of the fabled Garden of Eden. The deeds of real men began with the migration traditions from Hawaiki to New Zealand. The whakapapa of these founding ancestors are connected to myth figures such as Tawhaki and Rata. They range from fifteen to thirty generations, giving a time depth, in western terms, of less than a thousand years of human history. The contradiction is reconciled by the construction of some genealogies as tātai hikohiko. McEwen erroneously suggests that tātai hikohiko was a random selection of ancestors.[11] The words translate as a line of flashing lightning. This means, that far from being random, the genealogy was in effect a selection of luminaries.

Given the thousands of years of existence in tribal societies, it was not possible to record the names of all ancestors by oral transmission. Only the luminaries who had pivotal roles in the evolution and development of the Māori world were recorded in the whakapapa. Because genealogies were truncated, they were not absolute. They could also be lengthened, as they were in some tribal whakapapa, by the insertion of extra divisions in the epochs of creation, or deities in human lines to enhance them.

Tribal whakapapa were taught in schools of learning known as whare wānanga. The whakapapa were maintained by tohunga, who were recognised as professional genealogists. Their teaching was conducted in secret, under rigidly prescribed rules. Secrecy maintained the gap between priests and the uninitiated. The mystique was fostered by the use of archaic forms, obsolete words and guttural recitation. This prevented the whakapapa being captured by the uninitiated. In the celestial epochs of whakapapa, there was greater flexibility for the genealogist to exercise artistic licence by the insertion of poetic or compositional layers in the genealogy.

The poetic extension of whakapapa at the celestial level is evident in the Tainui tribes tracing the descent of their Hawaiki ancestor Ohomairangi from Tawhaki. There are ten levels in the genealogy. They are clearly metaphors for the procreative act of copulation between Tawhaki and Hapai.

Tawhaki = Hapai
Matire hoahoa   The enchanted wand
Rutu pahu   The resounding gong
Tangi pahu   The wailing gong

Ngā Pepa a Ranginui

Ngai	The panting sob
Ngai roto	The suppressed panting sob
Ngai peha	The proverbial panting sob
Hauraki ki te rangi	The dry heavenly breeze of summer
Mapuna ki te rangi	The pent-up love of heaven

Kuraimoana = Puhaorangi (celestial being)
Ohomairangi[12]

Tawhaki and Puhaorangi were celestial beings. Ohomairangi was their human descendant. From Ohomairangi there are four generations to the canoe ancestors Hoturoa of the Tainui, and Tama Te Kapua and Ngatoroirangi of the Arawa. These ancestors migrated to New Zealand some time in the fourteenth century. When they arrived, there were already tāngata whenua in possession of the land. From the archaeological record, we know that some of these prior inhabitants reached New Zealand towards the end of the first millennium. The later arrivals either intermarried with the earlier tribes, or conquered them, to produce new tribal formations.

In the case of the Arawa people, a peaceful beachhead was established at Maketu. But four generations after Tamatekapua, his descendant Rangitihi and his sons conquered the interior tribes and took over the Rotorua Lakes district. They established the tribal domain and defined its boundaries.

THE ARAWA WHAKAPAPA
Kuraimoana = Puhaorangi (celestial ancestors)
Ohomairangi (human ancestor in Hawaiki)
—
—
—
—
—
Houmaitawhiti (Hawaiki ancestor)
Tamatekapua (Captain of the Arawa)
Kahumatamomoe
Tawekemoetahanga
Uenukumairarotonga
Rangitihi

The whakapapa from the Hawaiki ancestors of the Arawa canoe to the traditions pertaining to Rangitihi's conquest of the interior of the North Island validated tribal mana and claims to land within their tribal boundaries. The sons of Rangitihi in their turn established the sub-tribes and marked out the subdivisions of territory. This process of arrival, settlement, conquest and tribal wars to defend territorial integrity spanned almost five centuries. The process was replicated by other canoe migrants over the rest of the country right up to the historic period ushered in by the arrival of Captain James Cook in 1769.

24 August 1993
(Paper delivered to the David Nichol Seminar IX, Voyages and Beaches: Discovery and the Pacific 1700–1840)

Taha Māori

TAHA MĀORI is a social concept based on descent from the aboriginal inhabitants of Aotearoa, who regarded themselves as tāngata whenua (people of the land). A basic component of Māori identity is the concept of Māoritanga, which incorporates ethnic traits such as skin pigmentation and cultural traits such as language, spiritual beliefs and identification with a particular tribe and geographic locality.

Māoritanga is difficult to pin down by a process of listing criteria as Ritchie attempted to do with his Māoriness scale of 1–10,[1] and Metge with her list of twelve characteristics for 'Māori ways'.[2] Paradigms of this kind are static, and as a consequence are difficult to match with the dynamism of human behaviour. Māoritanga is the analogue to culture, an equally difficult concept to define by listing what are thought to be its major characteristics, so for the purposes of this paper culture will be defined broadly as a design for living, and includes everything that is socially learned by the members of a society.

Ethnic features such as skin colour and hair form were

not components of Māori identity in pre-European times. Since the Māori were Polynesian, a hybrid sub-group of the Mongoloid, Caucasoid and Negroid divisions of human-kind, and had been isolated in the Pacific from 1500 B.C., they did not conceive of themselves as a race *vis-à-vis* other races. Instead, the Māori thought of themselves in terms of iwi. But with the arrival of European navigators, traders and missionaries, the Māori applied the descriptive term Pākehā (white man) to these strangers. Conversely, because white skin was a strange and abnormal condition to them they adopted the term māori (normal or natural) to distinguish themselves.[3] In this way, ethnicity became a component of Māori identity.

Traditions

The cosmogonic myths and stories of legendary heroes are located in a remote time and place of the fabled Hawaïki homeland. Traditions, on the other hand, are located in New Zealand and relate the doings of real men from canoe voyages to Aotearoa in the settlement of the land.

The ancestors of the Māori people settled the land they named Aotearoa from Central Polynesia around A.D. 900. They expressed their sense of identity and uniqueness as a people in the following aphorism:

> E kore au e ngaro te kākano i ruia mai i Rangiātea
> And shall never disappear the seed which was sown
> from Rangiātea.[4]

The early settlement phase was characterised by low population density with ample supplies of food obtained by hunting, fishing and gathering. But around A.D. 1100, a more sedentary existence developed around agricultural production, based on the successful transplantation of food crops from the Polynesian homeland.

The experimental phase which followed was character-ised by technical innovation in the propagation of the kūmara (*Ipomoea batatas*) from shoots, and controlled temperature storage to ensure survival of roots for the new season's planting in the spring.[5]

The development of systematic agriculture ushered in the proto-Māori phase characterised by settled papakāinga (villages) and pā. Food stores and property were accumulated in these villages. The food surplus allowed for increased specialisation of labour. Villages were now worth robbing so fortifications were built in their defence.[6]

As the population increased with agricultural production, cleared land became more valuable, and by A.D. 1300 the population had increased to 25,000.[7] This increased pressure on resources coincides with the appearance of large earthwork fortifications. One of the earliest pā, at Ōtakanini, near Helensville, is radio-carbon dated at A.D. 1351 ± 78, and the fortresses on the volcanic cones of the Auckland isthmus at A.D. 1430 ± 40. The canoe traditions of different tribes which Simmons associated with internal migrations because of population pressure in Northland emanate from this period.[8]

From the fifteenth century on, Māori traditions abound with accounts of tribal warfare over land. Warfare was the means by which tribal boundaries were defined and political relations between tribes established. Out of this period emerged forty-two tribal groups.[9] Tribal land boundaries were marked by physical features such as hills, rocks or prominent trees.[10] Land discovered by the founding ancestors and occupied for a thousand years was hallowed by ancestral bones buried there and blood spilt in its defence.

In time, the people came to think of themselves as being joined to the land as tāngata whenua. Prominent physical features on the landscape such as mountains, rivers or lakes were identified with founding ancestors and stood as symbols for a tribe. The following aphorisms express that symbolism:

Hikurangi is the mountain, Waiapu is the river and Porourangi is the ancestor.

Tongariro is the mountain, Taupō is the sea and Te Heuheu is the chief.

    Waikato of a hundred monsters, on every bend is a
    monster [chief].

Tribes differentiated themselves from one another on the
basis of the canoe traditions of the fourteenth century. These
traditions refer to the time tribes claiming descent from a
canoe ancestor became established as corporate groups.
These canoe traditions which emerged 400 years after the
first arrivals exist to validate claims to mana and land.[11]
Tribes took their designation from an eponymous ancestor
who was either on one of the fabled canoes or a descendant
of a revered canoe ancestor. An important feature of tribal
structure is its human scale. If a tribal group became too
large, there was a tendency for a younger brother of the chief
to split off a group of followers to establish his own hapū
(sub-tribe). Tribes with numerous sub-tribes took on a
corporate identity as a confederation of tribes under a paramount chief.
    From the point of view of an individual who was born
into a whānau, his social identity was derived from his membership in recognised corporate groups ranging in order of
size from the whānau, to hapū, iwi and waka.

History

While myth and tradition comprise the primary components
of Māori cultural identity, there is an historical dimension
as well. The Māori people had been isolated in Aotearoa for
close to 900 years when Captain Cook arrived in 1769.
Thereafter, frequent contacts with whalers, sealers, traders
and missionaries culminated in the recognition of ethnicity
as a component of Māori and Pākehā identity. Liaisons
between Māori women and Pākehā men provided the first
infusion of Caucasian genes into the Māori genetic pool.
Māori-Pākehā offspring were labelled with the pejorative
term half-caste by the Pākehā. But to the Māori, who
transliterated the term to hāwhe kāhe, there was no social
stigma attached. Indeed half-caste children were admired
for their beauty, a product of hybrid vigour. Because of

differing social attitudes to children of mixed unions, it was more common for these children to be identified with and socialised in their taha Māori (Māori dimension) than their taha Pākehā (Pāhekā dimension). This fusion between the two poles of Māori-Pākehā ethnicity is acknowledge by the aphorism:

Behind the tattooed face is another man
His face is white.

The coming of the Pākehā also opened up a cornucopia of material goods, which the Māori quickly adapted into their own culture. Nails, hoop iron and hatchets were in keen demand. This was the period of economic welcome to rangatira (chiefly) Pākehā, whose ships were laden with goods.

Māori control over trading relationships was short-lived. Strange diseases introduced by Pākehā seamen devastated the Māori population in some coastal areas in 1790 and again in 1810. The musket wars of the 1820s were even more debilitating. By 1835, the tribes longed for surcease and turned to the missionaries as the peacemakers. Church dogma, however, undermined Māori society by attacking important cultural symbols. Ancestral carvings were emasculated of their sex organs. In Northland, where the missions were first established, the art of carving disappeared altogether. Polygamy and slavery, two important buttresses of the wealth and position of chiefs, were abolished and the influence of chiefs thereby weakened. Customs considered to belong to the stone age such as tribal warfare, mākutu (sorcery) hahunga (exhumation) cannibalism, and tattooing of men were abandoned. Only the tattooing of the moko on some women persisted into the twentieth century. The missionaries who had become the trusted advisers of the Māori paved the way for the next stage in the erosion of Māori culture by advising the chiefs to sign the Treaty of Waitangi, on 6 February 1840.

Ngā Pepa a Ranginui
Alienation from the land

The Treaty of Waitangi paved the way for British imperialism and the eclipse of Māori mana by British sovereignty. Pākehā dominion was spread gradually over the land by the colonial techniques of extinguishing native title to land by fair purchase and the transmigration of surplus population from industrial England.

At first, the chiefs were willing sellers of huge tracts of land to Governor Grey's land-purchase agents. But when shiploads of settlers arrived to take up land, the chiefs sat down on the shore and wept as they watched the human cargo discharged on Aotearoa. They knew they were dealing with something much larger than the few thousand or so Pākehā who had settled among them. Competition for land and its resources transformed the relationship of economic welcome between Māori and Pākehā into opposition. Thereafter Māori and Pākehā became ethnic, social and cultural categories in a binary opposition of dynamic tension. That binary opposition is an important historical component in the contemporary definition of Māori identity.

20 June 1985

2: THE MEETING HOUSE

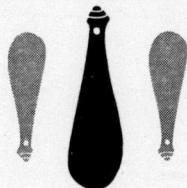

The genesis of the meeting house as a cultural symbol

THE ANCESTORS of the Māori arrived in New Zealand around A.D. 900. The early settlements consisted of small groups which obtained their food supplies by hunting, fishing and gathering. Initially, the settlements were temporary encampments consisting of crude shelters which could be moved according to the seasonal availability of food in different places.[1] By A.D. 1100, the settlements were stabilised in favoured localities as more substantial houses were built.

A site at Palliser Bay indicated that the typical Polynesian settlement pattern of a small village at the mouth of a stream, with cultivations on a sandy coastal platform, was well established by the twelfth century.[2] The first pit dwellings appeared at this time in association with underground food storage pits. The presence of these pits suggest that the Māori had solved the problem of growing some of the Polynesian food plants such as kūmara, taro, yam, gourd, and paper mulberry in the colder climate of their new home.[3]

Of particular importance was kūmara, the staple root crop. The kūmara needed a minimum storage temperature of 55–60 degrees Fahrenheit over the winter months, at 80 percent humidity, otherwise it spoiled.[4] The problem of keeping seed tubers for the new season's planting was resolved by the invention of the rua kūmara, the covered storage pit, lined with bracken.

The successful establishment of horticulture in the twelfth century ushered in the proto-Māori kāinga, or village settlements, which culminated in the development of pā Māori, the distinctive native fortifications. As a consequence of horticulture, the population increased and became more stable within favoured geographic locations. Cleared land became more valuable, food stores and property were accumulated, and fortifications were built in their defence.[5]

By A.D. 1300, the population had increased to approximately 25,000.[6] This increased pressure on resources – especially good horticultural land – coincided with the development of fortifications. Of the estimated 4,000–6,000 pā sites in New Zealand, 98 percent of them are associated with horticultural parts of the country.[7]

From the fourteenth century on, the tribal traditions abound with accounts of tribal wars. These wars, which were waged sporadically for almost five centuries into historic times, were the means by which tribal territories were demarcated and political relations defined. This was the period in which classic Māori culture developed and flourished up to the time of European contact.

The accounts of European navigators who visited New Zealand in the eighteenth century provide the earliest objective data we have on the dimensions of Māori houses at the time of European contact. Their observations were collated and tabulated by Groube, who concluded that the large communal meeting house was not a common feature in pre-European society.[8]

Observer	Date	Length	Breadth	Height
Cook	1769	20 feet	–	–
Banks	1769	18 feet	10 feet	5 feet
Monkhouse	1769	24 feet	16 feet	–
Monneron	1770	10 feet	5 feet	6 feet
L' Horne	1770	10 feet	5 feet	8 feet
Crozet	1772	8 feet	5 feet	–
Anderson	1777	33 feet	15 feet	5 feet

The houses were described in one account as being no bigger than a dog-kennel, with the doors being barely high and wide enough to admit a man crawling on all fours. They were seldom more than 16 or 18 feet long, 8 or 10 feet broad, and 5 or 6 feet high from the ridge-pole to the ground.[9]

From the observations of the early navigators, Groube concluded that the communal meeting house, which was such an important feature of Māori life in the nineteenth century, was not common in earlier times.[10] The large carved meeting house is, in effect, a post-European development. Groube postulates that the arrival of the missionaries stimulated the development and differentiation of the meeting house and marae complex.

The meeting house in mythology

Conceptually, the house as a symbol of rank, chiefly mana, and tribal identity is much more ancient than the nineteenth century.

In the twenty-eight stories of mythology and legendary heroes in the Māori text *Ngā Mahi A Ngā Tūpuna*, there are over 200 references to the word 'house'.[11] Similarly, in the Māori text of 189 pages by Nēpia Pohuhu, the major portion of which is taken up by genealogical tables, there are seventy-one references to house.[12]

According to Pohuhu, the deity Tānenuiarangi and his brothers journeyed specifically to Rangi-tamaku (the eleventh heaven) to fetch specifications from the prototype house in which poupou (carved posts) were assembled.[13] They took the measurements of the length of the ridgepole, the width of the house and its height. Tānenuiarangi then built a house named Matawhā because it had four windows, two in the front and two in the back wall. All the posts in this house were carved and decorated, including the ridge-pole, rafters, barge-boards, and central pillars.[14] In 1863, when Pohuhu wrote this story, fully carved houses, with both interior and exterior decorations, had just been built in the preceding two decades at Manutuke, near Gisborne, by Raharuhi Rukupo and other carvers of the Rawheoro school of learning. The description of the house, particularly the reference to carved rafters, fits exactly Rukupo's house Te Hau-ki-Turangā. Pohuhu's teachings are derived from the post-Christian Te Matorohanga school of learning which added the eleventh and twelfth levels of heaven to the earlier tradition of ten heavens. The story appears to be an attempt to provide a mythological charter from the celestial realm for the carved meeting house.

An examination of the Te Rangikaheke stories in *Ngā Mahi a Ngā Tūpuna* indicates that Pohuhu's later projection of current practice back in time served only to explain in detail the decorations of carved houses as they existed in the nineteenth century. The earlier myths had already described the carvings of decorated houses, their symbolism, dimensions and internal features.

When the demi-god Māui, who grew up in the celestial realm, returned to his family on earth, he was invited by his mother to stand on the ridgepole (genealogical descent line) of his ancestor Hinenuitepō's house.[15] This incident alludes to one of the conventions in the symbolism of the house as an ancestor whose backbone provides the main descent line of a tribe. Subsequently, when Māui fished up the North Island, his hook lodged in the door beam of his ancestor Tonganui's house. The house was described as having a porch and a carved figure above the barge-boards.[16]

In the story of the slaying of Tinirau's pet whale, both the noble Tinirau and the villainous tohunga Kae, who was responsible for the killing, had their own houses. Kae's house had a fireplace in it and was large enough to contain all his people, presumably a hapū of up to 300 people. The house had a carved centre-pole, which was the place of honour occupied by Kae himself. Although Tinirau's house also had a centre-pole, the two houses differed. Kae's house had a side entrance, whereas Tinirau's house had its entrance at one end.[17]

In the legend of Whakatau-Pōtiki, the enemy Ati-Hapai people had a house named Te Uru-o-Manono, in which the bones of his murdered brother Tū-Whakararo were hung on the ridgepole as a trophy. Whakatau avenged his brother

by burning Te-Uru-o-Manono while the whole of the
Ati-Hapai was assembled inside. One of the unusual features
of this house was that it had eight doors, which the investing
war-party had to cover to ensure no one escaped.[18] Thus,
the destruction of the tribe was synonymous with the
destruction of their house, the symbolic embodiment of their
identity. On the second of his missions to avenge the death
of Tuhuruhuru at the hands of Kae's tribe the Popohorokewa,
Whakatau burned their house Te-tihi-Manono as well. This
house was so large it had ten fireplaces in it.[19] Similarly, the
legendary Tawhaki, who destroyed the goblin-like Ponaturi
for killing his father, also completed his revenge by burning
their house Manawa-tāne.[20]

Clearly, in myths and legends, chiefs had superior
houses. The basic architectural elements of the chief's house
are cited in the stories. These included interior fireplaces,
the doorway in the front wall, the porch, which is such a
distinctive feature of meeting-house design, the barge-
boards surmounted by the carved human figure of a
tekoteko, the poupou, which are a feature of the interior
walls as both structural and decorative pillars, and the
poutokomanawa, the centre-post supporting the ridgepole.

While the tekoteko represents an ancestor, the ridgepole
is the line of descent. The centre-post supporting it symbolised the chief, the central figure in the tribe, and living
embodiment of the ancestors. The space at the base of the
poutokomanawa was where the chief sat as a mark of his
status as the pillar of the tribe. In the myth stories, the houses
of chiefs were large enough to accommodate their whole
tribe. In the wars between myth heroes and villains, the
defeat of an enemy was not enough. A victory was consum-
mated by the burning of the chief's house, the symbol of
tribal identity.

Myths are projections back in time of customary practices
and how people believe their institutions came into being.
They are set in the remote past and do not provide a time
scale when meeting houses, as described in the myths, were
actually built in New Zealand. Some myths, like the Pohuhu
account of Tānenuiarangi and his brothers copying the

dimensions of the prototype of a carved house in the eleventh heaven, may well be a projection back in time of what was happening in New Zealand in the post-contact period of the 1850s. In view of the prevailing architectural design of a rectangular house with a single window in the front wall, the story of Tānenuiarangi building a house with four windows is suspect as a post-European idea.

Although the first arrivals more than likely brought with them folk memories of large communal houses from their Hawaiki homelands in Polynesia, it is clear from Green's description of early settlements there was no evidence of substantial buildings. The first settlers were probably too preoccupied with survival in the new land to build and decorate large houses. But in the proto-Māori village stage of the twelfth century, when permanent settlements were established, there is a baseline of house construction from which house design and development can be traced up to historic times.

Māori dwellings of the classic period were described by Best as huts of about 10 to 12 feet long used for shelter and sleeping at night. But a larger house known as a whare puni was used by a community as a general sleeping-house.[21] A fuller description of Māori dwellings is provided by Buck.[22] Buildings ranged from lean-to shelters, houses without walls, walled houses, common houses of up to 20 feet in length, and superior houses. The superior houses formed two classes, whare puni or family sleeping-houses, and whare whakairo (carved house). Buck made no claim for the antiquity of the whare whakairo, other than to state that it was the peak of Māori artistic and architectural development. This paper is concerned with tracing the genesis of the carved meeting house and when the peak in development alluded to by Buck was reached.

The evidence of archaeology

The evidence we have about the design of prehistoric Māori dwellings is derived from archaeology. In the superior class of buildings, the whare puni was characteristically rectangular in shape. The length-to-breadth ratio ranged from 1.5 to 1 and sometimes 2 to 1. It had a very small door, and an extension of the roof and side walls at the front to form a porch. The internal plan consisted of a hearth or hearths down the centre and sleeping places or platforms down the sides. There were only minor variations from this basic form, which has a very long history in New Zealand.[23] This is because large houses, as we have seen in mythology, are linked to powerful behavioural and symbolic factors.

Proof of the antiquity and stability over time of the design of the whare puni was sought by Pricket in the excavation of the Moikau village settlement in Palliser Bay. The Moikau house he found had the expected length-breadth ratio of 1.52 to 1. The porch made up a quarter of the total length of the building.[24] This house put the development of the whare puni at approximately the twelfth century.

Sutton, who excavated the site of Pouerua in Northland, postulates A.D. 1300 as the time when the first houses were built there.[25] He identified four house types, to the first of which 'the phylogeny of the whare whakairo (carved house) can be traced over at least 500 years'. The type one houses, although not large, being up to 7 metres in length and 5.8 metres wide, characteristically had the highest gables. They had vertical walls, a stone-lined hearth, and a single door on the right side of the front wall. One example had a porch which was created by continuing the roof and side walls past the front wall. Type one houses were consistently oriented to magnetic north, unlike the lesser houses, where alignment varied according to peculiarities of the house site.

A salient feature of type one houses at Pouerua was a flat open space in front of the house. This space was at least as wide as the house, and varied in length from a third to the full length of the dwelling. The lesser house types did not have this space. Finally, the type one house and its courtyard were diametrically opposite the area where food was prepared, indicating the basic dichotomy between tapu (sacred) and noa (profane).

Sutton concluded that the type one house at Pouerua 'was the most potent symbolically of all dwellings present, that it was associated with individuals of status or rank. By implication, it was the prototype of the modern whare whakairo.' The claim is too bold. Sutton's type one house is of the same genre as Pricket's superior whare puni. There is a gap of 600 years between these prototype whare puni and the carved house that needs to be addressed.

Later examples of whare puni have been found at Makotukutuku, Palliser Bay and elsewhere. The Makotukutuku house, which was large enough to need two centre-poles, is dated about the fifteenth or sixteenth century. The ten poupou down the side of this house from the porch to the back wall consisted of squared timbers with notches at the top to bear the rafters.[26] Two larger houses dating from the eighteenth or early nineteenth century have been found at Te Awanga, and at Poor Hill, near Waimate North in Northland.[27]

Carved decorations

While the origins of the whare puni as the prototype of the architectural form of the meeting house can be traced in the archaeological record to the twelfth century, the time when carvings appeared is more difficult to define. The mythological origins of carving are attributed to an ancestor named Ruatepupuke, who fetched such knowledge from the domain of Tangaroa, god of the sea. Rua, who was a second-generation descendant of Tangaroa, was the mediator who transmitted the knowledge from the gods to later human descendants.

Clearly, Māori mythology claims great antiquity for carving. But because timber decays, carvings more than a few centuries old are not common. One of the earliest carvings that survived the ravages of time is the Kaitāia lintel, dated circa A.D. 1400 by Simmons.[28] The style of the tiki

The Meeting House

on the Kaitāia lintel reflects its Polynesian antecedents, especially its resemblance to Hawaiian carvings of Menehune (dwarf people). Isolation from the source in east Polynesia, with its basic designs of geometric surface patterns, led to the local development of curvilinear Māori art. The spiral pattern which distinguishes Māori art from the rest of Polynesia is found only in the Marquesas in the conventionalised ear, insect antennae, and on the knees of the tiki.[29] The inspiration for the curvilinear art of the Māori was the pītau, the centre frond of the tree fern.

While spirals and curved designs distinguished Māori art from the rest of Polynesia, its focus on the human form remained the same. The central motif of Māori carving is the tiki, which is relieved by embellishment with the manaia, the beaked figure, whose meaning has been lost in antiquity.[30] Motifs of lesser importance include birds, whales, lizards, fish, and sea monsters.

The time when tekoteko and carved door lintels appeared as decorative symbols on the exterior of whare puni has yet to be determined precisely. Since the Kaitāia lintel was meant to be viewed from both sides, and has a slotted attachment in the base, Simmons postulates it was a decorative roof-coaming rather than a door lintel.[31] Alternatively it could have been mounted on a post or a gateway. If the Kaitāia carving was a roof coaming, then it would be reasonable to assume that tekoteko and carved door lintels decorating houses followed soon after in the period designated by Mead as Te Tipunga, the growth period of Māori art from A.D. 1200 to 1500.[32]

By the time of European contact, in the eighteenth century, the primary elements of architectural design of the whare puni, with decorative carvings on both the interior walls and exterior barge-boards, were well established. Descriptions by Cook, Roux, and Crozet attest to the existence of carved central pillars in the houses, and carved poupou. One house seen by Cook and Banks at Tolaga Bay was 30 feet long and had all the side posts carved.[33] When the missionary Samuel Marsden arrived at the Bay of Islands in 1814, he was accommodated in a chief's house which was

30 feet in length. But the doorway was only 2 feet wide and 18 inches high.[34] Such a house was painted by Augustus Earle in 1827. This house, although no higher than the woman standing in front of it, is distinguished by its decorative tekoteko and carved door lintel, which mark it as a superior house. The house is notable also for not having a paepae, the beam dividing the threshold of the porch from the courtyard.[35]

It is clear from the descriptions of the early navigators that the kaupapa, or conceptual design elements of the whare whakairo, were present in the chief's house. While recognising that the chiefs' houses could have been the prototype of the meeting house, Groube advances the tentative hypothesis that it was a post-European development.[36] He suggests that the increase in size of whare puni was influenced by factors such as the availability of better woodworking tools, and the examples in size set by European houses and church halls. Another stimulus to the up-sizing of houses was the increase in the number of visiting Pākehā who stretched the hospitality of chiefs. This necessitated the building of larger houses solely for the accommodation of visitors.

The building of large houses to accommodate visitors was not unknown, however, in pre-contact times. The traditions of Ngāti Raukawa, for instance, relate that when their ancestor Wairangi and his 120 warriors journeyed to Ngāti Maru territory to recover his wife, who had absconded with Tupeteka, the visitors were housed in a wharau. This was a temporary shelter built especially for them. The house posts were of solid kahikatea saplings capable of holding the visitors entrapped, so they could be murdered.[37] On genealogical reckoning, this event occurred around A.D. 1600.[38]

In the traditions of the Tainui tribes, circa A.D. 1500, there is the celebrated story of the rivalry between the brothers Turongo and Whatihua for the hand of the puhi Ruaputahanga. During the building of his guest-house to receive Ruaputahanga and her entourage, Turongo was tricked by Whatihua into shortening the ridgepole of his house.[39] In the meantime, Whatihua built himself a large house, at a place which bears the name today of Wharenui. When the visitors arrived, Turongo's house was too small, and so the guests were accommodated in Whatihua's house. Needless to say, the latter won the hand of the virgin princess.

Although temporary guest-houses were built in traditional times, it is likely that the tempo of building, and size of such houses, increased with the arrival of Europeans. In 1820, Cruise described a newly built house as the largest he had seen.[40] It was specially built for white men who might want to stay in it. Polack noted that in standing villages, superior houses were built 12 feet from the ground to the ridgepole. These houses belonging to chiefs were 40 feet long and 20 feet wide.[41] One house built for Wakefield and his men of the New Zealand Company was 50 feet long and 28 feet wide.[42]

Response to colonisation

In the decade of the 1850s, as the flow of European settlers increased, tribal leaders in Taranaki began holding large assemblies to discuss ways of controlling settlement. The possibility of doing so by withholding the land from sale was one proposition discussed at such meetings among the Ngāti Ruanui. The numbers attending these meetings necessitated the building of large guest-houses. In 1852, the people at Katotauru built an immense whare puni named Kana a Kariri (Cana of Galilee). Such a large house had not been seen before by Woon, the local missionary.[43] In 1853, the Anglican missionary Richard Taylor found the people at Manawapou in Taranaki building another huge meeting house measuring 90 feet by 30 feet.[44] It was named Tai-porohenui, indicating that the tide of settlement would be stopped. The increase in the dimensions of a whare puni and the change in the ratio of length to width from 2 to 1 to 3 to 1 was an entirely new development in Māori house construction. These scaled-up houses, although not necessarily adorned in the interior, are the direct constructional antecedent of the large, modern meeting house. But, the ornamented predecessor of the carved meeting house, as alluded to earlier, was the chief's house.

With the introduction of iron tools in the eighteenth century, carving flourished. Elaborately carved pātaka (storehouse) displaced the waka taua (war canoe) as a status symbol between 1770 and 1820.[45] But in the next three decades, carved houses belonging to chiefs displaced the pātaka as the symbol of tribal mana. The transition from the pātaka to the carved house was evident in the increase in size of the chief's house, and the elaboration of its ornamentation. The house of the Tūwharetoa chief Iwikau painted by Angus in 1847 illustrated the trend. The height of the walls, and gabled roof, in contrast to the earlier house painted by Earle, had doubled. Although the barge-boards were plain, the conceptual design of the house portended the meeting house. The notable features of the house were the tekoteko and paepae. The latter feature, clearly absent in Earle's house, was introduced to keep out wandering pigs. The paepae, as the obvious place to sit when receiving visitors, gradually took on a ceremonial function which superseded its original purpose.

Te Rangihaeata's house Kaitāngata, painted by Angus in 1844, is a good example of a chief's house that looks exactly like a meeting house in its design and decorations. The maihi are plain except for the raparapa, the stylised representation of the fingers at the end of the welcoming arms of the ancestor. At the apex of the maihi is a tekoteko and below it a koruru. The latter is executed in the naturalistic style and is thought to represent Te Rangihaeata, the chief and master carver of the house. The amo are fully carved and appear to be about 6 feet tall, which would make the height of the house at the apex of the gable 12 feet. The house is notable for the 12-foot depth of its porch. These dimensions indicate that Phillips' estimate of 15 feet for the width of the house is an underestimation.[46] The house is much closer to 20 feet in width, which on the conventional ratio of length to width would give the house a length of 40 feet. The window and doorway are carved, with the lintel carving depicting two female forms flanking the spiral design. The female vulva are inimical to tapu, and their function is to neutralise any residual tapu on strangers entering the house. Apart from what appears to be a tiki, or carved centre-pole, which is partially visible through the doorway, we can only conjecture as to whether or not the interior poupou were carved. It is possible that they were not, since the poupou in the porch are not carved.

Other notable features of the house are the rafters in the porch, which are fully decorated with painted kōwhaiwhai designs, and the apparent absence of a paepae. There is some ambiguity on this point in the painting. Either the house is built on a platform, which would be most unusual, or there is a very low paepae on which the two amo stand, and the people depicted are seated. The ambiguity is heightened by what appears to be the outline of a tiki near the centre of what looks to be a paepae. Phillips is of the opinion that there was no paepae, but a painting of another house similar to Kaitāngata by Angus suggests that that opinion is wrong.

Another notable meeting house painted by Angus was built at Ōtawhao by the chief Puatia to commemorate the conquest of Maketu in the Bay of Plenty.[47] This house is very similar in its conception, design and decoration to Te Rangi-haeata's house. There are four major points of difference. Being viewed on an angle, the ambiguity of the paepae is resolved. There clearly is one on which the amo stand. A design feature of this house is the post at the front of the porch supporting the ridgepole. At the base is a tiki balanced by a tekoteko at the top. Both are carved in the naturalistic form in contrast to the koruru between them, which is stylised. Like Kaitāngata, the rafters in the porch of this house are decorated with kōwhaiwhai, but the poupou are not carved. It is possible the posts of the interior were plain as well. The maihi, too, are plain, except for the carved ends, which are done in the spiral instead of the stylised fingers. But the most startling feature of this house are the sculptural figures placed along the outside walls. On the right side of the porch, with only the top and bottom visible, is the zig-zag staff, symbol of wānanga, the school of learning where master carvers learned the esoteric lore of their craft. The sculptures of arms, heads and tiki along the visible side of the house parallel the placement of tiki along the poupou of the interior. But in this case, they are not ancestral figures. In the opinion of Pākariki Harrison, tohunga whakairo at Auckland University, they represent the slain and dismembered bodies of enemies, presumably from the conquest at Maketu.

One other house of this period painted by Angus in 1843 that merits some comment is Te Wherowhero's house at Raroera pā, near Te Awamutu.[48] It is an exception to the classic form of the whare puni, in that it is a whare kōpae, a house with a side entrance alluded to in the legend of Tinirau and Kae. Instead of a pair of gabled maihi, there is a single horizontal barge-board surmounting the two amo. The large carved slabs of the amo and the barge-board, combined with an estimated length of 40 feet or more, indicate it is a superior house, symbolising the status of its owner and his tribe. There are no other decorations evident on the door or the window, so it would be reasonable to assume that, like the other houses discussed above, it too might not have had carved poupou in the interior.

The most exceptional house of this period was that of Raharuhi Rukupo, named Te Hau-ki-Tūranga, which stood at Manutuke, eight miles south of Gisborne. Rukupo was born about 1800, and grew up during the time of a growing Pākehā presence in the land. As an adherent of Māori tradition, he was aware of the danger of cultural invasion. Rukupo opposed encroachment by Europeans in Poverty Bay, and the teachings of Christianity.[49] Rukupo, who was a master carver trained in the Rawheoro whare wānanga at Tolaga Bay, expressed his commitment to Māori traditions through his art. In 1842, as a cultural statement, and a counter to the Pākehā presence, he carved Te Hau-ki-Tūranga, a house that was completely decorated inside as well as outside. Although the house was built in memory of his brother Tāmati Waka Māngere, its name is evocative of tribal identity and mana. The name means vital force, essence, or sovereign power of the people of the district of Tūranga (Gisborne). The house is the prototype of the whare whakairo, which is decorated on the inside with carvings, tukutuku panels, and kōwhaiwhai patterns as well as exterior carvings.

Te Hau-ki-Tūranga is the only example of a chief's house from the 1840 period to remain intact to the present day. Unlike the other chiefs' houses at the time, its dimensions are accurately known. The house is 55 feet long, 18 feet wide, and its height is 11 foot 7 inches. The kaupapa, or conceptual plan of a carved house, functioned to conserve tribal history and genealogy, so that they would be communicated from generation to generation. To this end, fifteen ancestors are carved at the lower ends of the rafters, four on the poupou of the porch, and thirty-one on the interior poupou of Te Hau-ki-Tūranga.[50] The house is also notable for the two pillars supporting the ridgepole. The tiki at the base of the poutokomanawa is much thicker set than the one on the second post at the rear, signifying that ancestor's role as the powerful person holding the house and tribe together. With the use of iron and steel tools, Rukupo set a standard in the art of carving for subsequent carvers of houses to emulate. Rukupo's creative genius showed how the human form could, through imaginative design, be fitted into broader slabs of timber that had become available with new technology. The self-portrait of Rukupo on an epa (pillar on an end wall) inside the entrance of the house stands as a monument to the man, and testament to his creativity, which took the development of carved houses to the level of achievement that flourishes today in the modern meeting house.

Rukupo's fears about Pākehā encroachment were well founded. After the Land War in Waikato ended in 1864, guerrilla resistance by the Hau Hau dragged the war on in Taranaki. When the campaign spread to the East Coast in 1866, the Government threatened to confiscate land at Tūranga. But because the well-armed auxiliaries of Major Rōpata Wahawaha and Mokena Kohere intimated they would side with Rongowhakaata to resist confiscation, it did not proceed. Instead, Rukupo's house was purchased in 1867 by Richmond, Minister of Native Affairs, at a discount price of £150.[51] The house was taken to Wellington, refurbished and housed in the Dominion Museum as a national treasure.

Houses of protest

It is significant that the prophet Te Kooti, who was to carry forward the tradition of carved houses through the unsettling period of the New Zealand Wars, belonged to the same tribe as Rukupo. During his guerrilla campaign against the settler Government, Te Kooti had three large carved houses built for him. The adherents of his Ringatu faith built a house named Tānewhirinaki at Waioeka, near Ōpōtiki. A total of 196 pieces of carving have survived from this house. The carvings depart from traditional monochrome red paint to polychrome black and white and pink and white, showing a willingness on the part of Māori artists to innovate and use new materials brought by the European. The carvings are kept in storage at Waioeka waiting re-erection. The first attempt to rebuild the house in 1920 resulted in an aituā, the accidental death of the master carver, when the ridgepole fell on him. A second attempt to put the house up was also jinxed when the master carver died of a heart attack. These aituā are taken as signs that only a person of great mana, namely a descendant of Muriwai or Te Kooti, will succeed in rebuilding the house.

When Te Kooti hid out in the Urewera Ranges from soldiers who were hunting him, his Ringatu followers built a large house at Ruatāhuna, where they held meetings and church services. The house was named Te Whai-a-te-Motu to commemorate the pursuit of Te Kooti around the island by the military. The carvings were begun in 1870 and not completed until 1888. The Tūhoe and Ngāti Awa carvers who designed the kaupapa of the house concentrated on expressing their tribal origins, identity and traditions in the decor of the house. The central ancestors incorporated in the conceptual design included Toroa, captain of the Mataatua canoe, as the poutokomanawa of the house, and Toi-kai-rakau, the founding ancestor of the Bay of Plenty tribes. At the apex of the roof is the Tūhoe ancestor Te Umu Ariki. The house is notable for the use of painted carvings and pictograph decorations on the rafters. The pictures depict tree ferns, rātā, maire and miro trees so typical of the mountain domain of the Tūhoe people. Favourite birding trees are also illustrated, with hunters taking wood pigeons with their long slender spears.

In 1872, when Te Kooti became battle-weary from the unequal contest, he gave up fighting and sought refuge behind the aukati, the boundary line of the King Country. At Te Kuiti, he built a house named Te Tokanga-nui-a-noho, and gifted it to his Maniapoto hosts, who gave him sanctuary. The house was carved by a number of East Coast carvers, including Wiremu Kaimoana, of Ngāti Porou, and Apanui Hamaiwaho, of the Ngāti Awa tribe. The house is 75 feet long, 31 feet 10 inches wide and 21 feet in height. Originally, the house was thatched, as depicted in a photograph by Burton Bros. about 1888. A picture taken a year later shows the house roofed with iron and sheathed with weatherboard.[52] The conceptual design of the house stressed ancestral links between the East Coast and the Tainui tribes, by depicting Mahinarangi and Turongo at the base of the two pillars bearing the ridgepole. The Tūhoe and other tribes who supported Te Kooti are also represented among the twenty-eight carved poupou in the house. Canoe ancestors who link them include: Hoturoa (Tainui), Paikea (Ngāti Porou), Tamatea (Tākitimu), Tamatekapua (Te Arawa), and Toroa (Mataatua). This linking of founding ancestors from different tribes in a single house was a political statement on the need for a pan-Māori identity to counter the cultural invasion of the Pākehā. The carvings, like the ones in Tāne-whirinaki, are painted in polychrome red, black and white.

Fowler believes from missionary accounts that there were a number of carved houses in the Gisborne area that predated Te Hau-ki-Tūranga.[53] Te Poho-o-Rukupo, named after the master carver himself, was one such house. Others included Hamokorau, and Poho-o-Taharakau. No details are known of these houses except the statement from one of Fowler's informants that carvings from some of them were salvaged when they fell into disuse and were incorporated in Te Mana-o-Tūranga. This house was completed in 1883 to replace Te Hau-ki-Tūranga, near the original site at Manutuke.[54]

The conceptual design of Te Mana-o-Tūranga reinforced and elaborated the ideas laid down by Rukupo. Some of the carvings he did before his death in 1873 are incorporated in the house. As implied by its name, the house is a cultural statement, an assertion of Māori mana and cultural traditions, in particular, of the Rongowhakāta tribe. The carvings depict ancestral deities from the celestial realm of Te Pō, and tribal ancestors from the terrestrial realm of Te Ao Mārama (the world of light). Carvings on the maihi of the house illustrate the creation myth of Tāne's separation of earth and sky, and the myth of Māui fishing up the land. The legendary heroes Tawhaki and Rata are depicted on a post of the inside front wall. These myths are held in common by all tribes. But the carvings that depict ancestors from the terrestrial realm are confined to tribal ancestors of Rongowhakaata, Ngāti Porou, and Ngāti Kahungunu. These included Ruawharo and Tupai, who migrated from Hawaiki in the Tākitimu canoe, and Paikea, who crossed the ocean on a whale. Whole stories are incorporated in the carvings of Tutekohe and his dog, Tupurupuru's murder of the twins Tarakiuta and Tarakitai, and the story of how Porangahua fetched kūmara tubers from Hawaiki on the great bird of Ruakapanga. The love story that begat a whole tribe is depicted in the poupou of Kahungunu and Rongo-maiwahine. But not all posts in the house are ancestors. At the back wall of the house is a carving of a settler named Agnew Brown and his dog. This carving expressed not only the esteem in which Agnew Brown was held, but also incorporated the new reality of the presence of Europeans in the land.

Revival of carving

After Te Kooti, there was a hiatus in the construction of carved houses as Māori fortunes declined towards the end of the century. Tribal houses were still being built, but on a modest scale, or with little or no carving, as the art of carving all but died out. But as the population recovered from the nadir of 45,549 in 1900, and doubled over the next forty years, there was a return of confidence. This recovery coincided with the entry of Apirana Ngata into politics in 1905 as the member for Eastern Māori. Ngata sought symbolic expression for the recovery of Māori identity and cultural pride by promoting the art of carving and the building of carved meeting houses. For years he pressed the Government to support the school of Māori art at Rotorua run by the Ngāti Tarawhai master carver Anahata Rahui. But it was not until he became Minister of Māori Affairs that he succeeded in establishing the first national school of Māori arts at Rotorua in 1928.[55] The master carver Tene Waitere of Ngāti Tarawhai was the first tutor. He was followed by Eramiha Te Kapua. The first graduates of the school included Pine and Hone Taiapa of Ngāti Porou, Hēnare Toka of Ngāti Whātua, and Piri Poutapu of Waikato. These men were influential over the next four decades in re-establishing the art of carving meeting houses in their own districts as well as other parts of the country. They were also learned in the karakia and rituals associated with their craft. Piri Poutapu, for instance, taught his students the chants and offerings to appease Tāne for the felling of trees, rituals for the correct disposal of wood chips, and the taboos pertaining to food and sex during the carving of a house, as well as the mechanics and techniques of carving.[56]

Ngata began the renaissance of Māori arts and crafts by starting on his own ancestral house, Porourangi, at Waiomatatini. This house, which was opened in 1888, was moved by Ngata from the flood plain of the Waiapu River to higher ground in 1907. Everything, including the carvings, tukutuku panels, and even thatch were moved, refurbished and erected on the new site. Once the carving school at Rotorua was established, Ngata's promotion of the carved meeting house as the symbol of tribal pride and identity flourished. The opening of the carving school coincided with the plans of Te Puea Hērangi to build a carved house at Tūrangawaewae marae, the footstool of the King Movement at Ngāruawāhia. In 1927, Ngata arranged a fund-raising tour of Ngāti Porou territory for Te Puea's concert party Te Pou o Mangatawhiri. The tour raised £1,336 for the project. As a consequence of this intertribal co-operation, the house was named Mahinarangi, after the East Coast puhi who married the Waikato ancestor Turongo, thus commemorating the link between the tribes.[57] Ngata and Te Puea planned the opening of Mahinarangi in March 1929 on a grand scale that signalled the significance of the cultural revival to other tribes. Over 6,000 people from all tribes attended the opening and witnessed the action songs, haka, and poi dances.[58] As a consequence of this hui, the spread of the cultural renaissance was assured as the tribes returned home inspired to emulate what they had seen. Thereafter, Ngata's name became associated with many carved houses around the country, including Tākitimu at Wairoa, Tukaki at Te Kaha, Wahiao at Whakarewarewa, Raukawa at Ōtaki, Te Poho o Rawiri at Gisborne, and the Treaty Memorial House at Waitangi.[59] The carved churches at Tikitiki on the East Coast, and Putiki in Wanganui, also stand as testimony to Ngata's vision and the work of the master carvers he fostered through the carving school at Rotorua.

Urban marae

The carved houses built in the first stage of the cultural revival are symbols of tribal mana, and as such are located in tribal territory. But after the Second World War, when seventy percent of the Māori population migrated to urban centres in search of work, the meeting house as the most potent symbol of Māori identity and cultural pride was transplanted into towns and cities. While these urban houses serve the same traditional needs met by their rural counterparts, namely as a venue for tangihanga, weddings, and other ceremonial and community activities, they serve an integrative function as well for Māori living in an alien milieu. This integrative function is reflected by the organisational base underlying carved houses and urban marae. Some of them are traditional kin-based tribal marae, others are based on religious affiliation as the unifying principle, and others still are secular and multi-tribal, with an elected board of trustees. The conceptual design of the carvings in these houses reflects their integrative function in the choice of gods and ancestors that transcend tribalism. These houses, together with those which have been established in recent years by secondary schools and tertiary institutions, are all symbolic statements of Māori identity and cultural continuity in the face of the dominating presence of Pākehā in New Zealand.

3: THE TREATY AND TINO RANGATIRATANGA

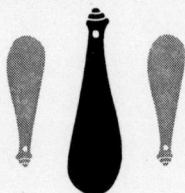

The Treaty of Waitangi as the focus of Māori protest

THE FIRST ARTICLE in the official English version of the Treaty of Waitangi sent to the Colonial Office purported to convey the sovereignty of the chiefs of New Zealand to the British Crown. The chiefs of the Confederation of the United Tribes of New Zealand, established by the British Resident James Busby in 1835, and the chiefs of the independent tribes outside the Confederation according to the Treaty:

> cede to Her Majesty the Queen of England, absolutely and without reservation, all the rights and powers of Sovereignty which the said Confederation or Individual Chiefs respectively exercise or possess, or may be supposed to exercise or possess over their respective Territories as the sole Sovereigns thereof.[1]

However, because of serious discrepancies between the translated Māori version of that key article and the English version, the Treaty is a morally dubious document. The Māori version of the first article when translated back into English reads:

> The Chiefs of the Confederation and all the Chiefs not in

that confederation cede without reservation to the Queen of England forever the Governorship of all their lands.

The moral validity of the Treaty hangs on the translation of the word sovereignty. The Rev. Henry Williams and Busby, who were responsible for translating the Treaty, were well aware that the Māori equivalent to 'sovereignty' was the word 'mana'. In October 1835, when Busby persuaded the thirty-five chiefs of the northern region to declare their national independence, the article of confederation was rendered as:

> Ko te kingitanga, ko te mana i te whenua o te whaka-minenga o Niu Tireni ka meatia nei kei nga tino rangatira anake i to matou huihuinga.[2]

> The kingship and sovereignty of the land of the confederation of New Zealand shall reside exclusively with the chiefs of our assembly.

Now, despite this clear association between kingitanga (kingship) and mana (sovereignty over land) in the article of confederation, the word mana is left out of the Treaty of Waitangi and the word kāwanatanga (governance) substituted instead. The historian Ruth Ross has criticised the translation of the Treaty for the use of 'missionary Māori', that is the use of missionary concepts and transliterations.[3] The word 'kāwanatanga' is a transliteration of governor into 'kāwana' which, with the suffix 'tanga', becomes governorship. Ceding governorship is not the same as ceding sovereignty. A governor is merely a satrap who rules on behalf of the sovereign. Furthermore, there were no governors in New Zealand as a referent by which the chiefs would have more readily understood the term. Their understanding of kāwanatanga would be understood as a benign term, not even remotely connected with the basic question of sovereignty.

But if sovereignty had been translated as 'mana whenua' (sovereignty over land), then the chiefs would have had no doubt as to its meaning. This being the case it is highly probable they would not have signed the Treaty. That the

Treaty did not appear to convey anything substantial to the Crown from the Māori viewpoint is encapsulated in the comment by the Kaitāia chief Nopera Panakareao: 'The shadow of the land goes to Queen Victoria but the substance remains to us.'[4]

The second article of the Treaty sets out Māori rights to the land and the exclusive right of the Crown to purchase the land should the Māori be predisposed to sell. The first part of the English version guaranteed the chiefs and tribes of New Zealand, and families and individuals

> the full, exclusive and undisturbed possession of their Lands and Estates, Forests, Fisheries, and other properties which they may collectively or individually possess.

The Māori rendering of this article guaranteed the chiefs, the tribes and all the people of New Zealand.

> te tino rangatiratanga o o ratou wenua, o ratou kainga me o ratou taonga katoa,
>
> the full chieftainship of their lands their homes and all their possessions.

The discrepancy of leaving out estates, forests and fisheries in the Māori version is indicative of the laxity with which the drafters and translators of the Treaty addressed their task. However, from the Māori viewpoint, this lapse is covered by the words 'taonga katoa' (all their treasured possessions). Both fisheries and forests are readily subsumed by the Māori meaning of these words. What is more important is the meaning that the chiefs would have taken from this guarantee. The word 'rangatira' means 'chief', which, with the appendage of the suffix 'tanga' becomes 'rangatiratanga' (chieftainship). Although this is a missionary neologism and also appears in the Lord's Prayer as 'kia tae mai tou rangatiratanga' (thy kingdom come), the missionary connotations of this word would not have affected the indigenous meaning within the context of the Treaty. Rangatiratanga over land is inseparable from the word 'mana'. So, from the Māori viewpoint, the guarantee of the rangatiratanga of their lands is equivalent to the guarantee of their sovereignty. Therefore as sovereigns under article 2, the chiefs ceded under article 1 to Queen Victoria in the person of her representative, Captain Hobson, the powers of a satrap. It is in this light that the comment by the Kaitāia chief Nopera Panakareao is more readily understood. 'The shadow (kāwanatanga, governance) of the land goes to the Queen, but the substance (rangatiratanga, i.e. chieftainship and mana), remains with us.'

Although some chiefs did not fully understand what they were conceding by way of kāwanatanga to the Crown, those under missionary tutelage knew. They had been warned by their mentors of the possibility of foreign intervention and advised that the lawlessness that prevailed in this Pacific frontier needed to be controlled by some form of government. It was the chiefs in the North most affected by the Pākehā presence, together with the missionaries, who sought British intervention. The cession of kāwanatanga, namely the right to govern the country, in the first clause of the Treaty is the charter for the establishment of the Governor and, ultimately, constitutional government in New Zealand.

The second part of article 2 of the Treaty gave to the Crown:

> the exclusive right of Pre-emption over such lands as the proprietors thereof may be disposed to alienate, at such prices as may be agreed upon between the respective Proprietors and persons appointed by Her Majesty to treat with them in that behalf.

The Māori translation of this section of article 2 is congruent with the English version so no further explanation is necessary. However, from the Pākehā perspective, the word 'pre-emption' is not entirely appropriate. The *Concise Oxford Dictionary* defines 'pre-emption' as 'purchase by one person etc. before opportunity is offered to others.' The Governor's application of pre-emption excluded other purchasers even if the Crown did not buy land that was offered.

Under the third article of the Treaty, Her Majesty the Queen of England, extended 'to the Natives of New Zealand

Her Royal protection and imparts to them all the Rights and Privileges of British subjects'. The Māori translation of this article is also congruent with the English version and needs no further explanation other than to say that the protection promised was against foreign invasion, and the rights and privileges of British subjects implied full equality.

Now the question arises as to how the uncontentious portions of the Treaty were accurately translated but the first article purporting to convey the sovereignty of the chiefs to the Crown was fudged by the use of 'kāwanatanga' instead of 'mana'. There are two reasons for this. In all the pre-liminary discussions with the missionaries concerning the need for British intervention to control their own nationals and to bring about peace and law and order between the tribes, the chiefs were universally adamant on one point: their continued right to the land. The missionaries knew that any loss of mana was anathema to the chiefs. Had the word 'mana' appeared instead of 'kāwanatanga' no chief would have signed. This proposition is asserted on the grounds that tribal wars in traditional times were fought over the assertion of mana and the maintenance of tribal and territorial integrity.

The second reason for disguising the meaning of the all-important first article of the Treaty was the vested interest of the missionaries in land. Colenso's account of the signing of the Treaty records that a white man accused the Rev. Williams of not translating accurately for the Governor charges by the chiefs concerning missionaries and their land acquisitions.[5] In his rebuttal, Williams denied having robbed the Māori of land. He said that in due course land titles would be examined by commissioners. He wished that to be done because he had a large family of eleven children for whom he had to make provision. Although he did not disclose the extent of that provision at the time, he subse-quently lodged a claim for 22,000 acres. He was eventually given a Crown grant of 9,000 acres, which was more secure and valuable to him than the original holding under the mana of chiefs.

On 5 February 1840, the northern chiefs as far south as

Hauraki assembled at Waitangi at the invitation of Captain Hobson to discuss the Treaty. It is evident from Buick's account that, despite the fudging of the meaning of the first article, the chiefs who spoke in opposition were clearly concerned over the question of mana. They did not want a governor if his presence meant a loss of mana for them. The chief Rewa told the Governor to return to his own country. He warned that the signatories would be 'reduced to the condition of slaves and compelled to break stones on the roads.'[6] Similarly, the Ngāti Hine chief Kāwiti told Hobson to return to his own country. Another chief named Tareha put the opposing viewpoint quite explicitly:

> We, we only are the chiefs, the rulers. We will not be ruled over. What! thou a foreigner up and I down. Thou high and I, Tareha, the great chief of the Nga Puhi tribes, low! No, no, never, never.[7]

Chiefs who spoke in favour of the Treaty included Hōne Heke, Patuone and Waka Nene. Heke confessed he did not understand the Treaty but put his faith in the advice of the missionaries. Waka Nene, who saw the coming of the Pākehā as irreversible, was the most persuasive speaker in favour.

> Friends! Whose potatoes do we eat? Whose were our blankets? Those spears [holding up his taiaha] are laid aside. What has the Nga Puhi now? The Pakeha's gun, his shot, his powder. Many of his children are our children.[8]

Nene indicated he would sign the Treaty. His elder brother Patuone endorsed what had been said and urged the Governor to stay and prevent a take-over by the French. The meeting adjourned at 4 p.m. and was to be reconvened again on 7 February. But because some of the chiefs had travelled a considerable distance and no food had been provided, they talked of returning home rather than waiting around for another day. Busby and the missionaries feared the chiefs would drift off without signing the Treaty so they advanced the meeting to 6 February. At 9.30 the next morning, there were over 300 people assembled in front of Busby's house at Waitangi. Over two hours passed before it was realised that no one had informed Hobson that the meeting had been advanced by one day.

By the time Hobson arrived, half the day had been lost. He came ashore so precipitately that he did not take the time to change into his uniform. Only his naval hat served as a symbol of his distinguished position. This mistiming of the whole affair probably accounted for Hobson's impatience. He would not countenance any further discussion on the Treaty and announced he was ready to take signatures. Despite Colenso's warning that the Treaty ought to be fully understood by the Māori to make it a legally binding contract, Busby called on the chiefs to come forward and sign. Hone Heke was called first and the signing commenced. A total of forty-three chiefs signed that day, twenty-three from the Confederation of United Tribes and twenty others. As each chief signed, Hobson shook hands with them saying, 'He iwi tahi tātou' (We are one people now). Colenso was given the task of giving each chief a present of two blankets and a quantity of tobacco.

The document signed at Waitangi on 6 February was regarded by Governor Hobson as the de facto Treaty. In the following five months, copies of the Treaty were taken by Hobson's emissaries to most districts in both the North and South Islands. Although 512 signatures of adherence to the Treaty were collected, the list was incomplete. In the centre of the North Island, the paramount chiefs Te Wherowhero of the Tainui and Te Heuheu of the Tūwharetoa confederations of tribes refused to sign. In acknowledgement of Te Heuheu's seniority, the chiefs of the Arawa confederation and some of the Tauranga chiefs refused to sign it as well.

One of the chiefs who signed at Waitangi was Iwikau, the younger brother of Te Heuheu. He had been on a musket-buying expedition at Waitemata when he heard of the meeting at Waitangi. For him, the acquisition of blankets by merely putting a mark on a piece of paper was too good to miss. He journeyed to Waitangi, signed the Treaty and collected two blankets. When Iwikau returned to Taupō with his blankets, Te Heuheu upbraided him for putting his mana under that of a stranger:

> I will not agree to the mana of a strange people being placed over this land. Though every chief in the island consent to it, yet I will not. I will consent to neither your acts nor your goods.[9]

Te Heuheu journeyed to attend a meeting at Rotorua convened by Morgan and Chapman to discuss the Treaty. There he returned the blankets accepted by Iwikau saying, 'Hau wahine e hoki i te hau o Tawhaki' (The power of a woman is negated by the power of a man). Despite not being present when the Treaty was discussed at Waitangi, Te Heuheu knew intuitively what was at stake. His refusal, supported by other chiefs, meant that the most populous Māori districts in the centre of the North Island were effectively outside the Treaty.

Despite the show of Treaty signing at Waitangi and other places, Governor Hobson issued two proclamations of sovereignty over New Zealand on 21 May. The first proclamation claimed sovereignty over the North Island on the basis of the Treaty signed at Waitangi and ratified subsequently by other chiefs. The second proclamation claimed sovereignty over the South Island by right of discovery, despite the fact that Major Bunbury, who had gone there to collect signatures, had not yet reported to Hobson. On his way back, Bunbury called in at Kapiti where Te Rauparaha signed the Treaty a second time. No doubt he would have signed it a third time had any other Pākehā offered him blandishments to do so.

What then did all this Treaty signing signify? A summation of those events which took place 147 years ago reveals it was an historic muddle. Captain Hobson, two of his officers and Busby all had a hand in drafting the Treaty. Hobson excised the florid language from Busby's draft before the final copy was handed over to Henry Williams for translation. The result of all this work is three English versions of the Treaty and a Māori translation which is not an accurate representation of any of them. Henry Williams was not the best scholar of Māori and he was assisted in the translation by his twenty-one-year-old son. The translation of sovereignty as 'kāwanatanga' disguised the true meaning of the all-important first article of the Treaty.

Both Busby and Williams are culpable of deception since they had used mana to signify sovereignty in their articles for the Confederation of Chiefs in 1835. Both wanted British intervention to bring law and order and to avert a possible takeover by France. Williams and other missionaries had a vested interest in their land claims, ranging from 1,000 to 50,000 acres.

Hobson, on the other hand, was clearly impatient. He was a naval man, unschooled in law, otherwise he should not have countenanced the contradiction of what was intended in the first article, namely the surrender of sovereignty, by the guarantee of rangatiratanga (chieftainship and therefore sovereignty) in the second article. Hobson's impatience ruled out further discussion the next day after the chiefs had time to think about the Treaty overnight. The signed Treaty would validate him as the undisputed governor of New Zealand, and he wanted that validation from the chiefs immediately.

It is also unfortunate that the signing of the Treaty was associated with gratuities. Iwikau and Te Rauparaha were clearly motivated by cupidity, but they were not the only ones. When the Treaty was hawked around the country, one chief at Otumoetai, near Tauranga, asked Major Bunbury how much he would get for signing. Others who saw it merely as a cash transaction put the matter succinctly, 'Pay us first and we will write afterwards.' 'Put money in my left hand and I will write with my right.'[10] Gratuities were a gross debasement of a serious transaction between two people by the glass-beads mentality of the colonial era. On the other hand, that the paltry material gain so readily seduced some chiefs into signing the Treaty casts serious doubt as to whether or not they fully understood its intent. The reduction of the Treaty to a crass commercial transaction lends credence to the cynical view of the opponents of the Treaty in the New Zealand Company as 'a praiseworthy device for pacifying the savages for the moment'[11] while men of affairs got on with the business of colonising the country.

While some chiefs signed the Treaty in ignorance, some for the gratuities and others out of the realisation that the coming of the Pākehā was inevitable, most would have signed because of the guarantee of rangatiratanga over land. In the preceding twenty years, the very foundations of Māori society had crumbled under the coming of the Pākehā. Introduced diseases and the musket wars debilitated Māori society. Chiefs could be laid low by commoners with muskets. New men trained in the mission schools as bearers of new knowledge were also a threat to the old order as were Māori seamen returning from abroad with new-found wealth.

The missionaries further undermined the position of chiefs by demanding an end to polygamy and slavery as a precondition for baptism. Both institutions buttressed the economic power of chiefs. The guarantee of rangatiratanga in a period of chiefly decline would have been an appealing reason for some chiefs to sign the Treaty. But we can only surmise at the number thus motivated since the chiefs did not record their thoughts in writing on this point.

Māori reaction

After the Treaty was signed and the pace of systematic settlement increased, the real meaning of the Treaty became manifest in the competition for land. In June 1843, Captain Arthur Wakefield enlisted the help of the police magistrate at Nelson and a posse of fifty armed settlers to enforce the New Zealand Company's claim to Māori land at Wairau. He was opposed by Te Rauparaha and Te Rangihaeata. Instead of waiting for Commissioner Spain to investigate the dispute, Wakefield attempted to bluff the chiefs into backing down by a show of force. A faulty musket in the posse discharged accidentally and the nervous recruits began firing at the Māori. A fight ensued in which nineteen Pākehā were killed, including Wakefield. This affray at Wairau was a clear signal to the Pākehā that Māori land was not there for the taking. Governor FitzRoy concluded the Company was in the wrong and he left the chiefs alone. In the meantime, there was growing disenchantment in the North. Hōne Heke, who had confessed to signing the Treaty in ignorance, found that the prosperity he had enjoyed before the Treaty declined. The imposition of customs duties by Governor FitzRoy drove ships away from the Bay of Islands, bringing free trade to an end. Revenue from land sales dropped as a consequence of the Governor moving his capital to Auckland and not having enough money to purchase land under the pre-emption clause of the Treaty. The situation was exacerbated by FitzRoy's imposition of a tax of ten shillings an acre on land sales.

Heke dramatised his disaffection in July 1844 by felling the flagstaff at Kororāreka and confiscating the customs signals. FitzRoy lowered the land tax to a penny an acre and replaced the customs duties with a property and income tax. In January 1845, Heke cut down the flagstaff again. The Governor then put out a reward of one hundred pounds for Heke's capture. For this insult of likening him to a pig that could be bought in the market, Heke cut down the flagstaff again in March and sacked the town of Kororāreka as well. FitzRoy sought to assert his mana by making war on Heke. He was not equal to the task and he was replaced by Governor Grey.

The advent of Governor Grey heralded the eclipse of Māori mana. His decisive campaign against Heke and Kāwiti pacified the North and brought it effectively under Pākehā hegemony. At that point in the development of the colony, Pākehā influence was confined to tiny beach-heads in the Bay of Islands, Auckland, New Plymouth, Wellington and Nelson. The major portion of the country defined as native districts was under tribal ownership and control. Grey had the resources to extend Pākehā dominion by a massive land-buying policy. Within the short space of ten years, his 'commissioners for the extinguishment of native title by fair purchase' had bought up the South Island, making good the Crown's claim to sovereignty. In contravention of article 2 of the Treaty, reserves of only ten acres a head were left to the impoverished Ngāi Tahu people.[12] The speed with which the South Island was taken over by the Pākehā was not easily repeated in the North Island, where the Māori population was much denser.

In the Hutt Valley, Grey resorted to declaring martial law to assert the land claims of the New Zealand Company against Te Rangihaeata. The classic technique derived from Roman times of building a road and erecting blockhouses was used to dispossess Te Rangihaeata and his people. As the settlers began to flood in to take up land purchased in the North Island at Auckland, Manawatu and Wairarapa, the chiefs perceived they were becoming a subject race as a consequence of the Government's acquisition of their lands. From 1853, intertribal meetings were held to discuss land sales. Gradually a consensus emerged around two basic concepts of kotahitanga (unification) and pupuri whenua (withholding land from sale).

This emerging sense of Māori nationalism was exacerbated by the establishment of the settler Government under the New Zealand Constitution Act 1852. The individual property qualification virtually disfranchised the Māori, negating the promised equality under article 3 of the Treaty. Furthermore, Grey took no steps to establish home rule in native districts as provided for under section 71 of the Constitution.

In the first twenty years after the Treaty, no resident magistrates were appointed in native districts. Left out of the machinery of government, untouched by the promised law and order of kāwanatanga and finally outnumbered in their own land, Māori nationalism fostered by the kotahitanga movement culminated in the election of Te Wherowhero as the first Māori King in 1858. The King, as the symbol of mana whenua (sovereignty over the land), was introduced by the chiefs to protect the land from further alienation.

Wiremu Tamihana, who facilitated Te Wherowhero's election, envisaged a conjoint administration with the King ruling over native districts and the Governor over Crown lands. But Governor Gore Browne took a jaundiced view of the King as a symbol of disloyalty to the Queen and a block to the acquisition of Māori land for Pākehā settlement. He was particularly exasperated by the fact that only seven million of the twenty-six million acres in the North Island had been acquired for Pākehā settlement. Europeans, he said, were determined to get the rest by correct means if possible, but if not then by any other method.[13]

In an ill-considered move, Governor Gore Browne made war on Wiremu Kīngi, who opposed the Government's partition of his land at Waitara. The injustice to Kīngi, who defended this right not to sell the land, impelled Bishop Selwyn to call for a judicial inquiry. Chief Justice Martin wrote a pamphlet on the Taranaki question in which he set out Māori land rights. He agreed it was not lawful for the Executive to use force in a civil question without the authority of a judicial tribunal.[14] A meeting of 3,000 Māori at Ngāruawāhia also called for a proper investigation of the Waitara dispute. The affair culminated in the recall of Gore Browne and the return of Governor Grey in October 1861 for his second term.

Grey brought the campaign in Taranaki to a conclusion in May 1863 then turned his attention to the Waikato. In July 1863, General Cameron invaded the Waikato. Grey's overt reason was to punish the chief Rewi Maniapoto for his part in assisting Wiremu Kīngi in Taranaki, but his real motive was to smash the King Movement. The Waikato campaign ended at the Battle of Ōrākau, just after Easter 1864. He followed this up with an invasion of the Bay of Plenty. Cameron suffered a severe defeat at Gate Pa. This was followed by a minor victory at Te Ranga, when sixty people were caught working in an unfinished fortification. Peace was made and the official Land Wars brought to an end.

To pay for the wars, three million acres of land were confiscated under the New Zealand Settlements Act 1863. These confiscations debilitated the King Movement, and the tribes of Taranaki and Bay of Plenty. But the conflict did not stop there. Guerrilla warfare was waged by the prophet leader Te Kooti until 1872 when he tired of the unequal contest. The prophet Te Whiti turned to pacifism, but even his movement was put down when his community at Parihaka was invaded and their houses smashed in 1881.

The Land Wars cost £3 million for the return of three million acres of land through confiscation. This was not a good return, so a more efficient way of getting the sixteen million acres still in Māori hands was devised through the establishment of the Native Land Court in 1867. The court functioned to transform tribal land from communal to individual title. Those named on the title to a block of tribal land were regarded as trustees by their people but were treated as owners by the law with power to alienate. They were readily seduced or suborned into conveying the title to land sharks and shyster lawyers by a corrupt process of advancing credit, fostering debts and threatening legal action for non-payment. The net result was wholesale dispossession of people of their patrimony. By 1960, only four million of the original sixty-six million acres of Māori land remained. The process of colonial despoliation set in train by Governor Gore Browne at Waitara had rendered the guarantees entered into by the Crown in 1840 at Waitangi as insubstantial as mist in the noonday sun.

Deputations to England

In the aftermath of the Land Wars, the tribes reorganised and held a series of meetings to discuss Māori rights under the Treaty. In 1879, the Ngāti Whātua chief Paora Tuhaere held a meeting designated as the first Māori Parliament at Ōrākei.[15] This meeting sought restoration of confiscated lands, curtailment of the Native Land Court and recognition of traditional rights to fisheries under article 2 of the Treaty. In 1881, the Ngā Puhi tribes met at Waitangi to analyse the articles of the Treaty and probe its meaning in the light of Māori misfortunes following its signing. This meeting concluded that, although the promised benevolence of the Crown had been withdrawn in the 1860s, it was not the fault of the Treaty. Therefore, the Treaty had to be taken back to its source, the Queen of England.

In 1882, the first deputation of chiefs led by Parore

journeyed to England to petition the Queen for redress under the Treaty of Waitangi for the wrongs perpetrated by the settler Government. Their petition cited the injustice to Wiremu Kīngi at Waitara, the unwarranted invasion of Waikato, the attendant land confiscations and unjust invasion of Parihaka. The petition sought a Royal Commission to draw out the Treaty from under the unauthorised acts of the New Zealand Parliament.[16] The deputation was treated evasively by Lord Kimberly and stonewalled by Lord Derby, the Secretary of State, who promised to lay their petition before the Queen, who would be 'pleased to receive it'. When the chiefs got back to New Zealand, they wrote the Treaty in stone and erected it as a memorial on Waitangi Marae to remind the Pākehā of his covenant, irrespective of the fate of the original paper document.

A second deputation led by King Tawhiao went to England in 1884. The petitioners cited the same grievances outlined by their predecessors. To this they added the Native Land Court practice of naming only ten selected persons on a certificate of title to a block of tribal land. The petition sought an independent commissioner from England to investigate Māori grievances. In June 1885, Lord Derby replied that the British Parliament was sympathetic and would intercede on their behalf with the Colonial Government. The failure of the two deputations to gain redress in England drove the chiefs to the conclusion that Māori solutions were needed for the problem confronting them. King Tawhiao established the Kauhanganui (Great Council) as a political forum for the Waikato, Hauraki and Maniapoto confederation of tribes. The tribes outside the King Movement formed Te Kotahitanga Mo Te Tiriti o Waitangi (Unity under the Treaty of Waitangi). This political federation, otherwise known as the Māori Parliament, held its first assembly in 1892 at Waipatu in Hawke's Bay.[17]

The Māori Parliament re-examined the Treaty of Waitangi to discover if there was any section in its articles that deprived the ninety-six chiefs in the assembly of their mana. Since the word 'mana' was not in the Treaty, they concluded it did not. They also concluded that under section

71 of the New Zealand Constitution it was lawful for them to proceed with their own parliament.

Despite the congruence of the policies put forward by the Kauhanganui and Kotahitanga calling for a Government review of Māori grievances, a cessation of road-making into Māori districts and a moratorium at the Native Land Court, they were ignored. In 1894, Kotahitanga, through the member for Northern Māori, succeeded in getting a Māori Rights Bill tabled in the House. The matter lay there indefinitely before it was rejected in 1896. This rejection made it clear that Parliament was not interested in sharing power with authentic Māori authorities such as Kotahitanga and the Kauhanganui.

The very thing that the chiefs feared in 1840 had, in the short space of sixty years, come to pass. Rangatiratanga was subordinate to kāwanatanga. The Government maintained the initiative by the Māori Councils Act 1900. The emerging educated elite of Buck, Ngata and Pomare were induced to support the Māori Councils' programmes in health and sanitation reforms on maraes. The Māori Councils were underfunded and so within ten years they were moribund, but by that time Buck, Ngata and Pomare had entered mainstream politics. Although these men promoted a cultural revival over the next twenty years, they did not seriously challenge the powerlessness of the Māori people arising out of colonisation and infractions of the Treaty.

The Treaty of Waitangi was taken up again in June 1914 by King Te Rata of the Tainui confederation, who emulated the odyssey of his ancestor Tawhiao to return the Treaty to its source. The deputation managed to obtain an audience at Buckingham Palace through the High Commissioner with King George V on the proviso it would raise nothing embarrassing. All the deputation got for its efforts was a promise from the office of the Colonial Secretary that their submission of Māori rights would be referred back to the New Zealand Government.[18]

Despite the failure of three earlier deputations to gain redress of Māori grievances under the Treaty, the prophet leader Rātana took another deputation to England in 1924.

The Rātana delegation was obstructed by the New Zealand High Commission and did not get an audience with the King or even the British Prime Minister. But Rātana did not give up. In 1929, he evolved a new plan to have the Treaty ratified so that its principles would be recognised in all laws relating to Māori people. In November 1934, Rātana's petition with 30,128 signatures to have the Treaty ratified by Parliament was tabled in the House by Tirikatene, the member for Southern Māori. The issue was held in abeyance for thirteen years before the Māori Affairs Committee passed a resolution in 1945 to have the Treaty printed and copies of it hung in the schools of the nation as a 'sacred reaffirmation'. This hollow gesture indicated that the colonial mind-set of short-changing the indigenous natives with glass beads had not changed after a century of interaction between Māori and Pākehā.

Statutory and judicial contradiction of the Treaty

As early as 1841, article 2 of the Treaty had been contradicted by the Land Claims Ordinance, which declared land not actually occupied by Māori as 'wasteland' and therefore property of the Crown. The Constitution Act 1852, which precluded communally owned land from the property qualification for electoral purposes, disenfranchised most Māori, thereby contradicting the promise of equality under article 3. Articles 2 and 3 were contradicted by repressive laws introduced during the Land Wars. These included the New Zealand Settlements Act 1863 for the confiscation of land from tribes 'deemed to be in rebellion', and the Suppression of Rebellion Act 1863 which suspended habeas corpus.

Although the Land Wars brought an increment of only three million confiscated acres to the seven million acres owned by Pākehā in the North Island, a further thirteen million acres was brought under Pākehā control by legal process. The Native Reserves Act 1864 placed all reserved native lands under Pākehā control through land commissioners and later the Public Trustee and Māori Trustee.

This measure was followed by the Native Land Act 1865 to establish the Native Land Court and the Native Land Act 1887, which allowed for the alienation of Māori reserves, completed the process of dispossession.

The passage of laws through Parliament which contravened the Treaty of Waitangi was matched by a series of Supreme Court judgements. As early as 1847, in the Crown v Symond (N.Z.PCC: 387), the Supreme Court ruled the Treaty of Waitangi was irrelevant. The only valid title to land emanated from Crown grant. But the most telling blow against the Treaty was delivered in 1877 by Justice Prendergast in the case of Wi Parata v the Bishop of Wellington. Judge Prendergast declared the Treaty to be 'a simple nullity'. The Crown's right to sovereignty was based in discovery and priority of occupation as New Zealand was occupied in the Judge's opinion 'only by savages' (3 NZ Jur (NS) SC 72). In 1939, that judgement was reinforced by Judge Myers, who declared the Treaty was enforceable only as part of municipal law and no legislative authority had been granted to the Treaty (NZLR 1939: 120).

The Treaty as a focus for nationhood

Despite a century of political, statutory and judicial denial of the Treaty, New Zealand's growing sense of nationhood sought symbolic expression through the Treaty of Waitangi. In 1940, the Centenary celebration at Waitangi was marked by the opening of a carved meeting house. In 1954, the visit by Queen Elizabeth II was marked by a highly ritualised celebration of Waitangi Day. In succeeding years, myth-making surrounding the celebration of Waitangi Day as the founding of a nation was backed up by a series of statutory provisions. The Waitangi Day Act 1960 declared 6 February as a national day of thanksgiving. The New Zealand Day Act 1973 made Waitangi Day a public holiday. But the change of name drew opposition from the Māori Council and so the Waitangi Day Act 1976 reverted the commemoration to the original name. Pumped-up ceremonies, like the affirmation to hang the Treaty in the classrooms of the nation, were a poor substitute for substantive action on Māori grievances as the Government soon learned to its cost. The 'celebration' of the Treaty became the focus of radical Māori protest action in 1971 when Ngā Tamatoa (The Young Warriors) proclaimed that unless the Treaty was ratified Māori would declare Waitangi Day a day of mourning. The Tamatoa protest was supported by a submission to the Government by the Māori Council citing fourteen statutes which contravened the Treaty. The Government, in keeping with its previous cosmetic responses to the Treaty, reacted by establishing the Waitangi Tribunal to hear Māori grievances. But the measure was not retrospective to 1840. Only infractions of the Treaty after 1975 when the Act came into force would be heard.

Even as the Treaty of Waitangi Act to establish the Waitangi Tribunal was being shepherded through the House, a 30,000-strong Land Rights movement marched on Parliament, demanding a moratorium on the alienation of the last three million acres of Māori land. The Māori Land March was followed by the occupation of disputed land at Bastion Point in 1977 and later other lands at Raglan and Awhitu. These events tended to bemuse the general populace, which failed to connect them with the Treaty of Waitangi.

In 1980, the Treaty was brought back into focus by the Waitangi Action Committee. It organised annual marches and protests to coincide with the Waitangi celebrations. As the protesters became more vehement each year, the Government responded by increasing the police presence at Waitangi to prevent the ceremonies being disrupted. In 1981, six protesters were charged with rioting for disrupting the investiture of Dame Whina Cooper and Sir Graham Latimer at Waitangi Marae prior to the Treaty celebrations. Although the riot charges were subsequently dismissed in the Kaikohe District Court, media distortion of protest activity left the enduring impression that the protesters were violent.

In subsequent years, the putative violence of the protesters created the opportunity for repressive police action. In 1983, the police arrested fifty people before they had got within the vicinity of the Waitangi celebrations. Another forty or more were arrested at the celebration itself. These people were detained for several hours without charges being laid and then released. In this pre-emptive strike, the police and their political masters had miscalculated the success of the Waitangi Action Committee in broadening their support. The arrest of a total of ninety-nine people without just cause, many of whom were Pākehā, served to raise the level of consciousness among the Pākehā populace about the fact that the nation needed to search its soul concerning the injustices of the colonial past. Four Pākehā clergymen who protested called not for celebration but repentance for injustice done to the Māori people.

In 1984, the Waitangi Action Committee succeeded in soliciting the support of two Māori movements founded in the last century, Kotahitanga and the Kīngitanga, in a hīkoi (peaceful walk) to Waitangi. The avowed intention of the hīkoi was to stop the Waitangi celebrations by a massive presence of people disapproving of the event. After the Pākehā experience of being detained without cause the previous year, the hīkoi was augmented by increased Pākehā support from HART (Halt All Racist Tours), ACORD (Auckland Committee on Racism and Discrimination), CARE (Citizens Association for Racial Equality), POW (People Opposed to Waitangi) and clergymen of various denominations.

As the hīkoi of 3,000 people advanced on Waitangi, the Governor-General as the Queen's representative departed from the politically and historically defined role of remaining aloof from aggrieved subjected people. He agreed to meet a deputation of 100 representatives from the hīkoi. The leaders of the hīkoi insisted that the whole hīkoi be admitted to the Treaty House grounds to meet the Governor-General. But the police halted the hīkoi on the open ground of the Waitangi reserve below the Treaty House and prevented what would have been an historic meeting from taking place.

The success of the hīkoi in mounting such a large demonstration of disapproval of the Waitangi celebrations in a manner that de-escalated confrontation with the police, and encouraged the Governor-General to take an independent position in relation to the hīkoi from that defined by the Government, demonstrated the futility of celebrating a dishonoured Treaty. This success was followed up in September by a national hui at Ngāruawāhia, the seat of the Kīngitanga, convened by Te Rōpū Whakawhanaunga i ngā Hāhi (The Māori Ecumenical Council of Churches) to discuss the Treaty.

As a consequence of the resolutions formulated by the thousand or so people who attended the hui, the Government changed the observance of Waitangi Day from a celebration to a more subdued commemoration in 1985. Before the House rose in December, the Treaty of Waitangi Amendment Act was passed to increase the Waitangi Tribunal's membership to seven and to give it retrospective power to 1840.

Tino rangatiratanga

TINO RANGATIRATANGA, which is currently the hot topic of discussion among Māori, is also the longest running. It has its roots in the chiefly rank system of pre-colonial times. The ariki, who were the paramount chiefs of large tribal confederations, traced their descent from ancestors who came to New Zealand on the migratory waka of the fourteenth century. Their genealogies also included celestial ancestors connecting them to the gods, thereby validating their right to rule in the manner of the divine right of kings.

Ariki were addressed as the personification of tapu, mana and ihi, the epitome of awesome, sacred, and sovereign power. Although such a notion of sovereignty had its genesis in the hierarchical rank system of Island Polynesia, it had to be reinvented in New Zealand. During the early phase of settlement, political landholding groups were hapū, led by rangātira. Although related chiefs could pull rank in terms of seniority of descent from canoe ancestors, in practice they regarded themselves as first among equals.

Hapū, like micro-states, fought each other in defence of territory, resources, and women. Hence the aphorism, 'Women and land are the reasons why men perish.' Eventually, warfare, combined with population increase, impelled related hapū to form iwi confederations under the leadership of ariki. In the Hawke's Bay-Heretaunga district, the chief Te Huki cemented his status as ariki by linking the Kahungunu tribes together in a series of political marriages for himself, his sons and daughters. These marriages were the 'seed bed of chiefs'.

Around Lake Taupō, the hapū of Tūwharetoa were beset by powerful enemies on all sides. To maintain their territorial integrity, a convocation of chiefs selected Herea as paramount chief to unify the east-west hapū divisions around the lake. The Te Heuheu dynasty sprang from Herea. The present incumbent, Sir Hepi Te Heuheu, is the seventh ariki to hold the title. He is a key player today as a rallying point for the sovereignty movement.

The emergence of paramount chiefs in different parts of the country signalled evolution towards a higher form of political organisation such as a monarchy. But the pace of its development was hastened by the process of colonisation.

In the Waikato region, the paramount chief Te Wherowhero of Ngāti Mahuta reinforced his mana by prowess in war. Although he was in his declining years when Pākehā settlers gained numerical ascendancy in 1858, he was seen as the rallying point for Māori nationalism. He was elected the first Māori King and took the title Pōtatau I. The King's function was to hold the sovereignty of the land on behalf of the tribes, and to stop the intertribal bloodletting. As the symbol of Māori nationalism, Pōtatau was a counterpoise to the Crown. He died soon after election and the onerous task of resisting British imperialism fell to his son Tawhiao.

In 1863, Governor Grey invaded the Waikato. The tribes outside the King Movement remained neutral as Tawhiao's kingdom was dismembered by the Imperial Army, and 1.2 million acres of land confiscated by the Crown. Despite the poverty and disempowerment that followed, the thirty-three hapū of Waikato stayed united in a protracted struggle with the Crown for justice. Tawhiao put a brave face on his oppression by proclaiming the independence of Māori as a sovereign nation in his newspaper *Te Paki o Matariki*. It was an act of faith that the tide of history would one day turn in Waikato favour.

The road to recovery began in 1910 when Tawhiao's descendant Princess Te Puea returned to live at Te Pou, Mangatawhiri, on the Waikato River. Her fund-raising efforts, through contract work, and travelling concert parties, culminated in the purchase of land at Ngāruawāhia, the former capital of the King Movement.

Te Puea and her followers cleared the land and established Tūrangawaewae Marae. Thereafter the Kīngitanga grew in strength from the time of King Koroki to the present incumbent, Dame Te Atairangikaahu. She is a fourth-generation descendant from Tawhiao and, like Sir Hepi Te Heuheu, is a repository of mana ariki, sovereignty that was never ceded to the British Crown. Neither of their ancestors signed the Treaty of Waitangi.

The King Movement's long-running land claim against the Crown, which culminated recently in the Tainui Deed of Settlement, is the high point of Dame Te Ata's reign. Although the return of 35,000 acres of land, and cash compensation of $170 million, barely does justice to the loss of land worth $6 billion, the settlement strengthens the mana ariki of Tainui. It also reinforces the Māori sovereignty movement in general.

Recently, Moana Jackson, an advocate of tino rangatiratanga, condemned the British assumption of sovereignty at a Commonwealth forum of non-governmental organisations in Wellington. This condemnation followed the demand by the Moutoa Gardens protesters for the Crown to enter into negotiations on Māori self-determination. The Prime Minister reacted by proclaiming that sovereignty was indivisible, there being 'one law' for all New Zealanders.

Despite Mr Bolger's pronouncement, sooner or later the Crown will have to address the issue of tino rangatiratanga. With republicanism in the offing, an accommodation will have to be reached where the Treaty will sit in a constitution. In anticipation of that event, papers on tino rangatiratanga have already been written by Matiu Rata, and Professors Whatarangi Winiata and Mason Durie.

Professor Winiata, who wrote the first paper in 1984, proposes a bicameral House. The lower house of representatives would be elected as at present. But in the upper house, tāngata whenua and Pākehā, as tāngata tiriti, will have equal representation. The upper house will have power to approve or block legislation from the lower house. This would ensure that no laws inimical to Māori or Pākehā interests will be passed.

A working model of this vision, instigated by Winiata, already exists in the Anglican Synod, where voting power between its Māori and Pākehā constituents is equal, irrespective of numbers. Only an arrangement of this kind will overcome the inherent flaw in democracy identified a century ago by Alexis de Tocqueville as the 'tyranny of the majority'.

26 June 1995
(*Metro*)

4: YOUNG TURKS
AND THE OLD GUARD

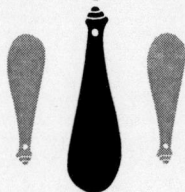

Tradition and change
in Māori leadership

PRE-EUROPEAN Māori society was characterised by kin-based corporate structures ranging in size from the whānau (extended family) to the hapū (sub-tribe), iwi (tribe) and waka. The waka was an ideological confederation of tribes based on one of the ancestral ocean-voyaging vessels that colonised Aotearoa from Eastern Polynesia in the fourteenth century.[1]

Leadership of these corporate groups was based on the principles of ascription and primogeniture, namely seniority of descent from founding ancestors. But these principles were not absolute. The model for juniors achieving high status is laid down in the exploits of the myth hero Māui. Ingenuity, skill, initiative, and bravery were just as important qualities for leadership as inherited mana and tapu from chiefly forebears. If they were lacking in a senior chief, then a junior assumed the mantle of leadership.

The leaders of the whānau were the kaumātua (male elder) and kuia (female elder). They made the decisions concerning the working of family land, the control and use of family property, and the rearing and education of children.[2] The kaumātua was usually the recognised spokesman on behalf of the whānau in the forum of the marae, the ceremonial courtyard of the village.

The hapū was the autonomous political land-holding group led by its own rangatira, descended from the ancestor after whom the hapū was named. It was comprised of related whānau and numbered between two and three hundred people.

The iwi was the largest kinship group. It was comprised of a number of related hapū, descended from a common eponymous ancestor.[3] Although the chiefs of the component hapū of an iwi could be ranked by seniority of descent, in practice they regarded themselves as first among equals. Among some iwi, with large territories and numerous hapū, ariki emerged as unifying iwi leaders. In the Waikato, and Tūwharetoa tribes, the ariki was selected by a convocation of hapū chiefs. In historic times, the office of ariki among these tribes became dynastic down to the present incumbents, Dame Te Atairangikaahu and Sir Hepi Te Heuheu.

Destruction of mana

In the nineteenth century, the external forces of European capitalism, missionaries, and British imperialism impinged upon, and progressively undermined the mana of, traditional leaders. The spiritual force of tapu, which controlled behaviour and buttressed the power of chiefs, was broken with impunity by visiting sailors from whaling and sealing ships.[4]

In the first four decades of the century, tribes were debilitated by European diseases and musket warfare. At this time, the missionaries became politically influential as peacemakers. From 1835 on, whole tribes began converting to Christianity because it was thought that the Pākehā God was more powerful than Māori gods. That power was manifest in the form of ships, weapons and an amazing array of goods possessed by Pākehā [5]

Conversion to Christianity eliminated the tapu of chiefs, thereby diminishing their authority. Chiefly mana was further eroded by the missionary demand to free slaves and put aside extra wives as a precondition of baptism.[6] Without slaves and wives to produce wealth, the chief's power to sustain the loyalty of his followers by exchange relationships was reduced.

With the erosion of chiefly mana, and a population loss of forty percent, Aotearoa was ripe for a foreign takeover. Under missionary influence, forty-one chiefs were persuaded to sign the Treaty of Waitangi on 6 February 1840.[7] The Treaty was subsequently hawked around the country and a total of 540 signatures collected. This aggregation of signatures, under the European convention of majority rule, undermined the mana of the three paramount chiefs who did not sign, Te Kani a Takirau, Te Heuheu and Te Wherowhero.

When Governor Grey took office in 1845, he used armed force to put down chiefs who resisted the colonial enterprise. They were excluded from the power structure of the state. Others were co-opted as subalterns to the Governor and ultimately the ruling class of the new nation state. The subalterns exercised functions of social hegemony and political government[8] as auxiliary soldiers, policemen, court assessors, public servants and politicians.

In the South Island, Governor Grey eliminated the mana whenua of the chiefs by extinguishing native title to land by 'fair purchase'. By 1863, the Crown had acquired the whole of the South Island.[9] 'Fair purchase' included coercion, threat of military invasion, and dishonouring promises to set aside reserves of 'tenths' from blocks of land sold to the Crown.

In the North Island, the chiefs organised to resist the colonial enterprise by withholding land from sale. The central feature of resistance was the election of a Māori King in 1859 to hold the mana whenua of the tribes.[10] In 1863, Grey made war on the Māori King to put him down. The tribes who supported him were debilitated by the confiscation of three million acres of land in Taranaki, Waikato and the Bay of Plenty.

With the eclipse of chiefly mana by state power, charismatic prophet leaders emerged to resist subordination.[11] Their mandate as leaders was derived from Jehovah, the archangel Gabriel, and the Christian religion. The prophets resorted to armed struggle, which extended the conflict to 1872. When it was clear that state power could not be overcome, the prophet Te Whiti turned to passive resistance and separation of the races. The Minister of Native Affairs, John Bryce, who was bent on asserting the hegemony of the state over Māori resistance, would not tolerate the prophet. He wrote a dark chapter in the history of New Zealand when he led the armed constabulary in the destruction of Parihaka in November 1881.[12]

In the aftermath of the Land Wars and subjection of the prophets, the chiefly leaders organised their own political response to state oppression. They were not enamoured of the four Māori seats in Parliament which were established in 1867. They characterised Māori MPs as 'tame parrots' for the Government in a Parliament of seventy members.[13] They were also concerned at the destruction of communal owner-ship of land and its alienation through the operations of the Native Land Court.

The adherents of the Māori King formed the Kau-hanganui, a Great Council, to seek devolution of control over Māori land from Parliament. Chiefs outside the King movement formed their own Māori Parliament for the same purpose. Both movements were ignored. By the turn of the century they were moribund. With their land base gone, the chiefs were disempowered.

Although Māori leaders today are still referred to as rangatira, the fundamental bases that underpinned the institution of chieftainship changed towards recognition of leaders by achievement as much as ascription.

Intellectual and organic leaders

After the turn of the century, the leadership initiative passed from traditional chiefs to leaders characterised by Gramsci as organic intellectuals.[14] These are the thinking and organising elements of a fundamental class, such as the Māori, who were subordinated by the Pākehā. At the forefront were the first Māori university graduates, Apirana Ngata, Peter Buck, and Māui Pomare. These men were intellectuals by profession.

Freire warns that educated men from subordinate strata are determined from above by a culture of domination, which constitutes them as dual beings. But they are necessary to the reorganisation of the new society, for which purpose they have to be reclaimed by the revolution.[15] In the case of Ngata, Buck and Pomare, their people reclaimed and validated them as political leaders. They were selected by customary procedures for three of the Māori parliamentary electorates.

The ruling class accepted these intellectuals as deputies, to exercise what Gramsci has termed subaltern functions of social hegemony and political government.[16] As long as they performed that function, their positions were secure. They were not concerned with pursuing Māori sovereignty as the chiefs did before them. Ngata, for one, accepted the Pākehā historical narrative of the transference of Māori sovereignty to the Crown as a *fait accompli* under the Treaty of Waitangi.[17] He did not raise the moral question of the disguised meaning of sovereignty as kāwanatanga (governance) in the first clause of the Treaty.

Ngata and his colleagues were essentially reformists who worked for the physical and cultural survival of their people. To this end, they instituted health reforms, revived Māori arts and crafts, and started Māori land development schemes using state loans. For carrying out these functions of social hegemony and political government, they were honoured with knighthoods. But when Ngata began empowering his own people by replacing Pākehā supervisors of the schemes with Māori ones, public servants in Native Affairs turned against him. The schemes were attacked in the press as a 'ghastly sink' for Pākehā money.[18] In 1934, when a Commission of Inquiry found that two of Ngata's appointees had falsified scheme accounts for personal gain, Ngata resigned as Minister of Native Affairs.[19]

While the intellectuals tried to resolve Māori problems from within the parliamentary system, there was growing poverty among the people who had no land. As their plight was exacerbated by the Depression, they turned to charismatic Wiremu Tahupōtiki Rātana for salvation. Like the prophets who preceded him, Rātana's role as a leader was validated by God. As an organic leader, Rātana turned his 20,000 followers into a political force by selecting candidates to contest the four Māori seats. He aligned the three seats won by his candidates at the 1935 election with the Labour Government. Ten years later, he delivered the fourth seat as well.

The Rātana-Labour alliance brought no substantial benefits to Māori apart from the general benefits of the welfare state. The reason for this poor outcome was the subaltern role of Māori members within the Labour Party and in the overall political structure. They were outvoted within their own party, as well as in Parliament. The Rātana-Labour alliance ended after forty years when Matiu Rata resigned from Parliament to launch his own Mana Motuhake (Māori sovereignty) Party in 1980.

New institutional mandates

After the turn of the century, the establishment by the state of new institutional structures such as incorporations, tribal trust boards, Māori Councils and the Women's Welfare League, provided additional platforms for the validation of both intellectual and organic leaders. These institutions were problematic in that they were created by government sanction. Those that were constructed as statutory bodies were given limited functions related to economic management, social hegemony and political government.

Māori land incorporations were fostered by Ngata under section 122 of the Native Land Court Act 1894. Incorporated owners elected their own management committees of between three and seven members. The committees formulated management plans for grassing, fencing and stocking land. Although incorporations were concerned primarily with economic development, they provided power bases for aspiring political leaders. But they were not perfect, because power in incorporations, like public companies, is wielded by major shareholders. Those with no shares have no say.

They, along with minor shareholders, become alienated from the land by having to seek employment outside their tribal territories.

Tribal trust boards were established by the Crown to receive compensation money for confiscated land, fisheries or the expropriation of lake beds. Because all members of a tribe were beneficiaries, trust boards were a better mechanism for validation of tribal leaders than incorporations. But the 1955 Māori Trust Boards Act definition of board functions – to promote education, health, social and economic welfare – indicates their subaltern role in maintaining social hegemony. That hegemonic role was made even more explicit in the Hunn Report suggestion that the cause of Māori education would be advanced if it could be laid down, preferably by agreement, that half their income be devoted to education.[20]

In 1900, the Government blunted the challenge of the Kauhanganui and the Māori Parliament by establishing Māori Councils. The statute ensured the councils carried out state goals of political government and social hegemony by giving them low-level, non-political tasks. These included such matters as improving Māori health, marae sanitation, discouraging tohunga, and ensuring compliance with new building standards for meeting houses. After ten years, when it was deemed that the political threat from chiefly leaders had receded, financial support for the councils was withdrawn and they became moribund.

The Māori Council system was revived under the Māori Social and Economic Act 1945 and revamped under the Māori Welfare Act 1962. Leadership in this quasi-autonomous national government organisation was validated by a four-tiered elective process based on parochial committees, executives, district councils and a national council. This bureaucratic structure, derived from Pākehā models, sat uneasily over kin-based corporate groups of whānau, hapū, and marae committees. Although the Māori Council was separated from its predecessor by half a century, its underlying agenda of political government and social hegemony was the same. The Māori Council and its subsidiaries were expected to promote the social, economic, cultural, educational and spiritual advancement of the people. Like its predecessor, the Māori Council was not fully funded for the task.

The Māori Women's Welfare League, which was formed by the Department of Māori Affairs in 1951, also had a four-tiered structure like the Māori Council. This is not surprising, since the department had a central role in the construction of both bodies. Unlike the Māori Council, the League is not a statutory body. Its *raison d'être* is the care and nurture of children. Consequently, the League has made a contribution to early childhood education through the development of playcentres and kōhanga reo.

As state-fostered institutions, the Māori Council and the Welfare League provided legitimating bases for intellectual and organic leaders, both within and outside tribal territories. But, as subalterns within the power structure of the state, they were expected to co-operate with its bureaucratic systems of control and management of the people. Any leader who deviated from that role was perceived as a subversive and marginalised in political discourse as a radical. Those who conformed to the role defined by the rulers were awarded Royal honours and granted additional but limited powers.

Urbanisation

The rural-urban shift of 75 percent of the Māori population in the second half of this century had a profound effect on Māori leadership. Urbanisation increased Māori knowledge of metropolitan society and its techniques of domination and political control. The crucible of the urban milieu threw up a new generation of organic, radical, Māori leaders who created their own platforms, political networks and supporters. They engaged in a counter-hegemonic struggle by deconstructing the historical narrative of the coloniser, and mounting protest actions and demonstrations against social injustice.

In the vanguard were Ngā Tamatoa, Matakite, the

Waitangi Action Committee, and Te Rūnanga Whaka-whānaunga i Ngā Hāhi. Their efforts, in the decade of the seventies, culminated in the empowerment of the Waitangi Tribunal in 1985 to address historical injustices, and thereby the rewriting of history. This change, combined with the inclusion of clauses relating to the Treaty of Waitangi in twenty-one statutes, raised the Treaty to the level of a constitutional instrument. Of particular import was the inclusion of Māori fishing rights, guaranteed by the Treaty, in section 88 of the Fisheries Act 1983.

The dynamic thrust of radical Māori politics in the seventies politicised a wide range of people to participate in the struggle for emancipation. It even empowered Māori subalterns within the Department of Māori Affairs to adopt a more proactive Māori position in the formulation and implementation of programmes. The discourse between community leaders and officers of the department at Hui Whakatauira in the early eighties culminated in the two innovative projects of kōhanga reo and Hui Taumata.

The kōhanga reo, which started as a pre-school language recovery programme, became one of the most dynamic political movements of the eighties. Over a thousand people attended the first national conference of kōhanga reo in January 1984. In the struggle for resources to establish 700 or so kōhanga reo, Māori women empowered themselves by taking control of the pre-school education of their own children. In doing so they learned to deal with bureaucracy and put pressure on primary schools to establish bilingual programmes to ensure language continuity for kōhanga reo children. Eventually, some kōhanga reo protagonists moved to establish the preferred option of kura kaupapa Māori. There are fourteen established kura kaupapa with another fifty-five community groups waiting approval for their kura.

The Hui Taumata 1984 was a Māori economic summit conference that signalled the desire for a Māori-controlled bank to invest in Māori business. The first attempt by the Secretary of Māori Affairs to initiate the bank by borrowing $600 million offshore precipitated the so-called 'Māori loans affair'. The scheme was aborted. In 1988 it culminated in the abolition of a department that was getting out of hand. Control was restored by replacing it with the Iwi Transition Agency, whose brief was to mainstream (i.e. assimilate) Māori programmes over a five-year period and go out of business. The agency was disestablished before its term was up and replaced by Te Puni Kōkiri in 1992. One of the ironies of the situation is that this department is known as the Ministry of Māori Development, at a time when it is not delivering programmes to the people. It was perhaps a Freudian slip that the designation 'puni' for 'ministry' also means 'to block' or 'stop'.

The grand scheme of the Hui Taumata, to establish a Māori bank, was scaled down to a Māori Development Corporation with a capital base of $26 million. The Government contributed $13 million, the Māori Trustee $7 million, Fletcher Challenge $2 million and Brierley Investments $2 million. This body, known as the MDC, provided a new platform for Māori leadership initiatives. Although it is a state-created corporation, the selection of its board takes cognisance of ascription as well as achievement criteria.

The chairman of the board of MDC is Robert Mahuta, who has a unique combination of mandates as a leader. His primary mandate stems from his aho ariki, his aristocratic descent line in the Tainui confederation of tribes. His hapū, Ngāti Mahuta, constitutes the heart of the Māori King Movement. He is also a graduate and an organic intellectual who has exercised enormous influence in the development of his people. The other member on the board representing iwi interests is Georgina Te Heuheu, a graduate in law with a tribal mandate from Tūwharetoa.

The chief executive of MDC is Waari Ward-Holmes. He achieved success in the corporate world of business and was strategically placed when the corporation was formed to become its first chairman. Although ethnically Māori, Ward-Holmes was not part of the struggle that led to the establishment of the corporation. When the chief executive resigned because of conflict over Māori values, Ward-Holmes had to decide whether his loyalty lay with his colleagues in the business fraternity or his people. He chose the latter, who then validated him as a Māori leader by endorsing him as chief executive.

In the MDC, Mahuta and Te Heuheu represent the mana of the two tribal confederations whose paramount chiefs did not sign the Treaty. The living repositories of that mana are Dame Te Atiarangikaahu and Sir Hepi Te Heuheu. In June 1989, Sir Hepi initiated an intertribal hui at Tūrangi, which culminated a year later in the formation of the National Congress of tribes. The Congress, being iwi based, ruled out the Māori Council and the League, the two pan-Māori national bodies that had held centre-stage in cultural politics for almost four decades. The sole purpose of the Congress is to provide a national forum for iwi to address cultural and political issues within tikanga Māori[21] and formulate policy recommendations to the Government. Delegates to Congress are nominated by their iwi. Because Congress refrained from distinguishing between iwi and hapū, it is a large body comprised of sixty-two iwi, fourteen taura here (urban iwi affiliates), and twenty-five rūnanga. With the formation of this body almost a century after the Māori Parliament was formed, the Māori struggle for empowerment had gone full circle.

27 July 1993
(Inaugural lecture, Te Wānanga o Tāmaki, University of Auckland)

Wild cards

MĀORI MEMBERS of Parliament are the wild cards of New Zealand politics. They can no longer be relied upon to act conventionally in terms of the old dichotomies between National and Labour, Māori and Pākehā. The post-election uncertainties of a ruling party with a wafer-thin majority of one were dispelled by the member for Eastern Māori, Dr Peter Tapsell, crossing the floor of the House to accept the post of Speaker.

A conservative by inclination, Tapsell sits more comfortably with National than Labour. According to one of Tapsell's colleagues in the medical profession, he liked the trappings of power, the ministerial car, the driver, the deference, and the pomp and ceremony. He was stunned when it all came to an end at the 1990 election. Now he has made the most improbable of political resurrections to resume the trappings of office which befit his conception of himself as a rangatira.

The other political wild cards are Winston Peters, Sandra Lee and Tau Hēnare. The also-rans are Koro Wētere and Whetu Tirikatene-Sullivan. They failed to sniff the winds of political change and chose to remain institutionalised within the Labour Party.

Peters is undoubtedly the most charismatic of the present crop of New Zealand's politicians. He generates good copy for journalists, communicates succinctly on television, and, like that master politician Sir Robert Muldoon, exudes an animal magnetism that captivates his audience. But unlike his former mentor, Peters does not have the animus to go for the jugular, or stomp on an opponent who is down. Journalists are forever trying to second-guess Peters, and they invariably get it wrong. The reason is simple. Peters is a sophisticated, highly educated, bicultural person. The journos try to psyche him as a Pākehā. They cannot deal with the duality of his persona as a Māori.

As the member for Tauranga, Peters has portrayed himself as the consummate politician. Like a chameleon sitting on a white rock, Peters made his political reputation defending the private property rights of his Pākehā constituents from the seemingly unreasonable and endless Māori treaty claims. He quickly rose to the top of the preferred Prime Minister stakes. But when he found himself sitting on a brown rock as Minister of Māori Affairs, the chameleon delivered what his portfolio demanded, a brown policy called Ka Awatea. Its manner of launching, combined with his criticism of his Government's financial policies, got him offside with his caucus colleagues. His expulsion followed, with the inevitable formation of New Zealand First as the party for the Peters' constituency among super-annuitants and disaffected Nationals.

Although New Zealand First is firmly rooted in main-stream politics, the party's first political success came from the unexpected quarter of Northern Māori in the person of Tau Hēnare. He came from nowhere to defeat the lack-lustre incumbent, Dr Bruce Gregory, and the veteran campaigner Matiu Rata. Hēnare's good looks, the magic of his family name, and the optimistic confidence of a young man out to conquer the world are a potent combination. His election was orchestrated where the numbers are, in suburban Auckland. The rural votes were pulled in by his name and that of his leader, Winston Peters. These two between them have broken irrevocably the long-standing allegiance of Māori voters to Labour in Taitokerau.

The other Māori wild card on the political scene is the attractive and intellectually potent Sandra Lee. She wrested Auckland Central from the incumbent member, Richard Prebble, for the Alliance. Lee has been a long-standing member of Matiu Rata's Mana Motuhake Party, which took her into the Alliance. However, there is not a large Māori population on Waiheke Island where Lee lives. Accordingly, she had to build her political support among Pākehā who elected her as an Auckland City Councillor. There she cut her political teeth on environmental concerns and saving the islands of the Hauraki Gulf from foreign purchase. Lee's debut on the local body scene coincided with a move among disaffected Labour supporters in Ponsonby and Freemans Bay wanting to oust Prebble for his part in dismantling the welfare state and the sale of state assets. Nancy Prebble's eleventh-hour denunciation of her husband also helped.

Sandra Lee, who comes from the South Island, belongs to the small Poutini clan of Ngāi Tahu on the West Coast. She has been a long-time opponent of the leadership of Tīpene O'Regan, chairman of the Ngāi Tahu Trust Board. Now that Lee is ensconced in Parliament the Trust Board will be more accessible to her, and O'Regan may have less room to manoeuvre than he once had.

As for the also-rans, they are a spent force politically.

Wētere has no future in politics other than making up the Labour numbers, in a situation where the rules of the game have been irrevocably changed by the advent of MMP. Whetu Tirikatene-Sullivan is in the same boat, as was made abundantly clear when her colleagues failed to support her nomination to chair the select committee on electoral law reform. Talk of injured pride, sexism and racism is hogwash. Her Labour colleagues were still in the two-party mode of business as usual. They failed to grasp the opportunity to exercise consensus politics by electing a chairperson who was not a member of the governing party. Tirikatene-Sullivan was readily placated with an apology extracted from her Caucus colleagues by Helen Clark. She has been so institutionalised by Parliament that she failed to seize the moment in history to walk out of Labour with her constituents and attach them either to Alliance or New Zealand First. They are the parties of the future under MMP.

In the meantime, the independent variable of Māori politics in the run-up to MMP is the Māori electoral option. There are 290,000 potential Māori voters, but 140,000 of them are on the general roll, while 40,000 are not enrolled at all. These voters have only until 14 April to get on to the Māori roll if they want to increase Māori representation up to seven seats under MMP. The onus is now on Māori, both committed and 'born again', to stand up and be politically counted.

25 February 1994
(*Metro*)

Sir Graham Latimer – political survivor

SIR GRAHAM Latimer is a political survivor. He has been a member of the Māori Council for thirty-two years, a long-standing Māori Vice-President of the National Party, and chairman of the Taitokerau Māori Trust Board. In recent times, Sir Graham copped criticism in all three positions. He surrendered the Māori Vice-Presidency of the National Party only because it was supposed to rotate. Like many such posts, the office became so identified with the incumbent that his re-election was taken for granted until potential challengers called for the exercise of the retirement rule. Even then, he was allowed one more term on the understanding he would not stand again next time round. Many Māori have an aversion to putting an eminent person down by the anonymous power of the ballot box.

Sir Graham had humble origins. His father worked on the Auckland wharves. His Pākehā mother imbued him with the values of pride, thrift and self-confidence. He was always on the make.

After the war, Sir Graham went to Japan in the J Force. It was at this time that he met and married my cousin Emily. I remember him fronting up, bold as brass, to my aunt and mother, the dowagers of our tribe, to ask for her hand in marriage. He was not fazed by their Catholic objections to his Anglican faith. Having done the decent thing by announcing his intentions, he took their daughter off anyway, and married her in the Anglican Church.

After demobilisation, Sir Graham worked for New Zealand Railways as station master at Te Hana. From there he went to a dairy farm at Tinopai which he won by ballot under the Returned Services Rehabilitation scheme. He was a successful farmer who worked on the principle of 'farming for production instead of profits'. In 1962, he joined the Māori Council, and ten years later became chairman. This position, combined with his Vice-Presidency of the National Party, and chairmanship of the Taitokerau Trust Board, enabled Sir Graham to become a financial wheeler and dealer.

When National reclaimed the Treasury benches from the Rowling Government, Sir Graham got sufficient funding for the Māori Council to run a secretariat and pay himself an honorarium of $30,000. For this he was criticised by district councils who thought the money should have been devolved to the grass-roots. He drew more opposition during the 1981 Springbok tour and was lucky to survive a motion of no confidence for attending the reception for the team at Gisborne. Thereafter there was a concerted move in the

thirty-three member council to unseat him. Sir Graham sub-
verted the move by bringing in three extra votes through
the formation of a new district council in Hauraki. Despite
that gerrymandering, he was shaken at having survived by
only one vote.

When a high-quality dairy farm came on the market at
Taipuha, Sir Graham's connections in the corridors of power
enabled him to finance its purchase and quit the more
isolated property at Tinopai. He expanded his holding by
purchasing an adjacent property when it came on the market.
Now a millionaire in his own right, Sir Graham schemed to
establish an economic base for the Māori people. As the
leader of a national organisation, he was often placed in the
invidious position of having to guarantee overdrafts on the
Māori Council's bank account for the payment of wages,
travel, and office overheads pending the receipt of the
Government grant.

The first scheme to make money by launching Māori
International on the takeover of the Māori Arts and Crafts
Institute at Rotorua was almost aborted by Arawa opposition. The public relations in the Māori world were so badly
handled that the Muldoon Government could not devolve
the institute to MI. It was an idea before its time. Although
MI traded its way through the 1987 crash, its annual profits
hovered modestly around the $70,000 mark.

As a political opportunist, Sir Graham piggy-backed on
the successful Muriwhenua fishing claim before the Waitangi
Tribunal to bring an injunction in the High Court against
the Government's Fisheries Quota Management system. The
injunction succeeded, and the Crown made an *ex-gratia*
payment of $1.5 million, which Sir Graham banked in the
Māori Council's account. This action miffed Tīpene O'Regan,
leader of the Ngāi Tahu fisheries claim. However, the bulk
of the money paid the legal costs of all claimants and enabled
them to continue negotiating with Government. The
negotiations culminated in the Sealord settlement of the
Māori fisheries claim. The negotiators, Latimer, O'Regan,
and Rata, had arrived as the first members of the Brown
Table.

Although not a runaway success, the MI experience gave Sir Graham a taste for putting deals together. In 1990, he managed to purchase the former THC Waitangi Hotel on behalf of the Taitokerau Trust Board for $600,000. That was followed by the purchase of the Rural Bank building in Whangārei for $20 million. His modus operandi in a trust board that had a financial base of only $71,000 was simple, if not reckless. Borrow 100 percent, get hold of the asset and let the cash-flow take care of the loan. He also put together a $10 million stake on behalf of Māori trust boards in the QUINZ consortium to buy the Quality Inns chain. This deal caused a rumpus behind the scenes when some of the trust boards defaulted on their promissory notes and the Māori Trustee as guarantor had to cover for them.

Two of the Taitokerau Trust Board deals went sour. It lost on the South Pacific Fibre Company in Whangārei, and a timber mill. In Parliament, Sir Graham came under fire from Ross Meurant and John Carter, who called for an inquiry into the affairs of the board. Among the Ngāti Hine in Northland, there were rumblings of no confidence in Sir Graham. Despite that, he survived a meeting of Trust Board beneficiaries. Perhaps the theatrical media transmission of mana from Dame Whina to Sir Graham helped. But the Pākehā world was not so forgiving. The mud thrown at Sir Graham was sufficient reason for his removal from the board of QUINZ. It may be a portent of things to come.

25 March 1994
(*Metro*)

Chainsaws and sovereignty

THE STATEMENT by Simon Upton in a newspaper column that the British Crown, and subsequently the New Zealand Parliament, 'effected a revolutionary seizure of power' not ceded by chiefs at the signing of the Treaty of Waitangi, is an admission of what Māori have known all along.

The Minister of Justice, Doug Graham, went one step

further by saying that the Government's sovereignty was based on successful British colonisation rather than arguments over what was legal, or even moral and just. That is an even graver admission, because a society not founded on justice and high moral principle will not endure.

The genius of the British, as they set about the business of colonising and dominating the indigenous people of the new world, was their ability to convince the natives that they were the torch-bearers of civilisation and justice. In the nineteenth century, it was the missionaries who persuaded the chiefs to petition the British Crown for a Governor to give them laws, to administer justice, and to protect them from foreign powers.

For the first two decades, the Treaty was a good deal. Chiefs and their tribes welcomed immigrants for the goods and capital they brought into the country. The Māori economy prospered, supplying food for New Zealand Company settlements, and raw materials for export. Thereafter it all went wrong.

By 1858, immigrants outnumbered tāngata whenua. Māori were politically marginalised by having no representation in Parliament. Then, in 1860, the Governor embarked on a war to assert the sovereignty of the Crown over independent tribes. The colony was in a turmoil as the struggle for supremacy dragged on for twelve years. In the Waikato campaign, the Imperial Army suffered two major defeats, at Rangiriri and Gate Pā. But that did not deter them. One of the characteristics of British genius has been the capacity to lose battles, yet end up winning the war. As the late Sir Keith Sinclair wrote in *A History of New Zealand*, 'the white man's peace was more devastating than his war', as Parliament set about the business of oppressing Māori and expropriating their resources. Down the years, well into this century, petitions to Parliament to redress injustice fell on deaf ears.

Despite colonial despoliation, the game has not ended. Urbanisation saw the rise of Māori activism led by Tamatoa in the seventies, the Waitangi Action Committee in the eighties and Ahi Kā in the nineties. Ahi Kā is an ancient concept, meaning domestic fires burning on the land to signify occupation and ownership. The term was adopted by the founding members of Tamatoa, Syd and Hana Jackson, to signify Māori sovereignty. The concept of Māori sovereignty was defined in this remarkably prescient statement written by Donna Awatere in a 1982 issue of the feminist magazine *Broadsheet*:

> Māori sovereignty is the ability to determine our own destiny and to do so from the basis of our own land and fisheries. In essence, Māori sovereignty seeks nothing less than the acknowlegement that New Zealand is Māori land.

Land and fisheries are the very resources that Māori have argued for with some success in the Waitangi Tribunal and the High Court. The $150 million Sealord deal, and the recent Tainui settlement of $170 million, are the outcome. But it is only the beginning, because for Māori the struggle for reparations from the state, particularly the return of land as the footstool of sovereignty, is a matter of survival. Awatere states succinctly why the struggle will be relentless and unremitting: 'Without sovereignty, we are dead as a nation. It is not sovereignty or no sovereignty. It is sovereignty or nothing. We have no choice.'

Mike Smith had no choice when he chainsawed the tree on Maungakiekie to dramatise Māori opposition to the fiscal envelope, the attempt to settle $18 billion dollars worth of land confiscation with a paltry $1 billion. Ken Mair had no choice but to occupy Moutoa as a proclamation of the sovereignty of his people's 'whanganuitanga'. Tama Iti, who tussled with Ian Fraser on television, had no choice but to campaign for the return of 2,000 ha of Tūhoe land confiscated in 1866. That land is needed as the footstool for the sovereignty of Te Mana Motuhake o Tūhoe.

Awatere was right. Māori who identify as Māori have no choice but to align themselves with the Māori sovereignty movement as Annette Sykes has done. As a professional person qualified in law, Sykes has made it in the world. Although young, she has already distinguished herself with appointments to directorships in Moana Pacific Fisheries and Māngai Pāho, the quango administering Māori Broad-casting funds. Theoretically, she could have opted for a peaceful life and risen to even dizzier heights. But as a Māori, it is not an option. Her genes have aligned her with the struggle and not the Establishment.

As the intellectuals in the Māori sovereignty movement, Sykes and Smith have targeted the sale of land and state assets to foreigners as a threat to Māori aspirations. They reason that by the time parochial leaders have their claims processed by the Waitangi Tribunal the Crown will have divested itself of assets with which to settle claims. Accordingly they made use of last month's Asian Develop-ment Conference in Auckland to warn off foreign investors. They warned that if the resources for the maintenance of Māori sovereignty continued to be eroded by sale to foreigners, their investments would not be secure. Forests might burn, and dams be blown up, as happened in other parts of the world where indigenous rights have been trammelled.

Predictably, the Prime Minister, Jim Bolger, condemned Sykes and Smith as anarchic 'self-appointed' leaders, thereby misconstruing the enduring nature of the Māori struggle for self-determination, and the growing strength of the sover-eignty movement. Māori are in it for the long haul, and sooner or later the Crown has to come to terms with it, especially with Doug Graham and Simon Upton's admission that Māori sovereignty was taken in the first instance by revolutionary seizure of power.

12 May 1995
(*Metro*)

Te Heuheu is the man

SIR HEPI Te Heuheu is the man of the moment, the most influential Māori leader of our time. He is an ariki, a man of breeding, the closest thing we have in New Zealand to royalty. Sir Hepi is a direct descendant of Tūwharetoa, the founding ancestor of the tribe whose domain surrounds the inland 'sea' of Taupō. His canoe ancestor was Ngatoroirangi, the priest navigator of the Arawa canoe. Beyond Ngatoroirangi, Sir Hepi's lineage extends back in time a thousand years to culture heroes of the fabled Hawaiki homeland of the Māori, and beyond that to the gods of the celestial realm and the creation of the cosmos. These celestial ancestors validate mana ariki in the manner of the divine right of kings. The respect which Sir Hepi is accorded by Māori is encapsulated in the aphorism 'Tongariro is the mountain, Taupō is the sea and Te Heuheu is the man.'

The founder of the Te Heuheu dynasty was Herea, circa 1800. His son Te Heuheu was a man of such great power and prestige that he was accorded the honorific name Mananui. In 1840, when Governor Hobson's emissary invited Te Heuheu to sign the Treaty of Waitangi at Rotorua, he refused, saying, 'Hau wāhine e hoki i te hau o Tawhaki.' This allusion to mythology was a definitive statement that cession of mana to the British Crown was not negotiable, notwithstanding the power of the British Empire and the monarch who straddled it. Sir Hepi, who is the inheritor of the sovereign power of Mananui, is the seventh ariki of his lineage, hence his title Te Heuheu Tukino VII.

As a descendant of Mananui, Sir Hepi has kept faith with his ancestor's tradition of standing aloof from the Crown and its manipulation of subaltern Māori leaders. It helps that his tribe kept their lands intact and amassed a fortune in forestry, tourism, and a wide array of business investments.

Sir Hepi is a private man, shunning the limelight for most of his life. He first came to public attention in 1984 when the Hīkoi, the peaceful march to Waitangi, was stopped by the police from meeting the Governor-General, Sir David Beattie. On that day, Sir Hepi adopted the humble role of mediator, relaying messages between the protest leaders, police, and the Governor-General. Humility is one of the hallmarks of the breeding of an ariki.

Although the meeting with the Governor-General did not eventuate, Sir Hepi picked up on the mood of the people. They would not bend to the will of the state by compromising their principle of group unity and allowing a select group to be split off to meet Sir David Beattie. Their affirmation of independence, and non-compliance with an agenda defined by state power, was in keeping with the traditions of his own forebears. It encouraged him to take a more proactive role in national Māori politics outside the concerns of his own tribe.

As the decade of the eighties drew to a close, the battle between Māori and the Crown over land and fisheries claims was well joined. Although the claims were largely tribal, most tribes were submerged by the aggressive capture of the discourse with the Government by a quartet of prominent Māori leaders. Those leaders were in turn captured by the Government's designation of them as negotiators, a kind of Brown Cabinet with which the Government could negotiate a politically feasible settlement. Sir Hepi responded to this co-option of Māori leaders by convening a hui of tribal leaders that culminated in the establishment of the Tribal Congress at Tūrangawaewae Marae in 1990.

The Congress espoused the principles of kotahitanga (unity), mana motuhake (discrete power), and tino rangatiratanga (tribal sovereignty) as its basic tenets. Membership of the Congress is limited to tribes, thereby excluding government-sponsored bodies such as the Māori Women's Welfare League and the Māori Council. Congress funds itself by levying its members $5,000 per annum, thus maintaining its independence from the Government.

As the new boy on the block, Congress was marginalised in the development of the Sealord deal that settled the Māori fisheries claim. By the time thirteen tribes came out in opposition, it was too late for Congress to intervene. The episode confirmed the need for the independent stance from the Government staked out by Sir Hepi, and the need to subject state-defined policies to critical scrutiny before complying with them.

When the Government unveiled its treaty settlement policy with a fiscal cap of $1 billion, Sir Hepi called a hui of over a thousand Māori leaders at Tūrangi. The hui rejected the fiscal envelope as a breach of 'tino rangatiratanga' and called on the Crown to stop the sale and disposal of assets over which Māori have rightful claims. The Minister of Justice, Doug Graham, who had scheduled thirteen hui of his own to discuss the policy with tribes, called the hui misguided. That was a misjudgement, an affront to the mana of Sir Hepi and the esteem in which he is held as the symbol of Māori aspirations to national sovereignty. Predictably, the thirteen hui were a public-relations disaster for the Government as tribe after tribe rejected the fiscal envelope with extravagant theatrical gestures of defiance.

The Government, as heir to the colonial traditions of domination, control, and manipulation, has not yet adapted to the multiple discourses of the post-colonial era. Its comprehension of the Māori view of reality is as myopic as that of its predecessors. Occupations of land and buildings followed at Moutoa Gardens, Tamaki, Huntly and Takahue as individual tribes asserted their tino rangatiratanga. These collisions between the tribes and the state are the result of starving the Waitangi Tribunal of resources to deal with the log-jam of small claims, and the Government's preoccupation with direct negotiations to settle a few large claims within its fiscal envelope.

Last month, Sir Hepi convened another hui of over a thousand people at Hirangi Marae. The hui affirmed the tino rangatiratanga of each tribe and established a working party to prepare proposals for constitutional reform that would include the collective tino rangatiratanga of the tribes. Unless this issue is addressed by the Prime Minister, with Sir Hepi as the mediating power, civil disobedience such as the conflagration at Takahue will continue to disturb the equanimity of the nation.

25 September 1995
(*Metro*)

5: FIGHTING OVER FISH

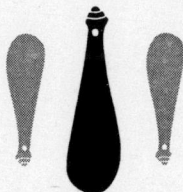

Goods in the sea

THE TREATY of Waitangi is a document that recognised and guaranteed aboriginal property rights to
land, the sea and its resources around New Zealand
coastal waters. If the Māori were willing to sell all or part of
those rights to the colonising British, they were extinguished
by 'fair purchase'.

In 1840, the Ngāti Whātua chief Apihai Te Kawau sold
3,000 acres of land on which the city of Auckland stands to
Governor Hobson for £200. A year later, Hobson sold
portions of the land for over £24,000. Although the deal was
a steal, Te Kawau acknowledged the validity of the sale at a
hui at Ōrākei in 1879 when he said, 'The land I sold, but the
sea I did not. Some of my goods are there.' The significant
thing about Te Kawau's statement is the assertion that his
rights to the sea, guaranteed by treaty, were still extant. The
reason for that assertion was the expropriation of the sea
and its resources by the Crown and the circumscribing of
Māori rights by various laws such as the Oyster Fisheries
Act 1869, The Fish Protection Act 1877 and the Harbours
Act 1879.

Apihai Te Kawau's assertion of ownership of the sea
began the long fight by Māori people to reclaim it. A search
of records by the Waitangi Tribunal found ninety-three
petitions by tribes and individuals complaining to Parliament about the usurpation of their rights by the Crown.

Although the Crown was warned by the Native Land Court that its control over the shores of New Zealand was subject to customary usage and Crown title would not be complete without extinguishment of native title, it continued on its chosen course. The consequence of that cavalier treatment of Treaty guarantees is collision in the courts over Māori fisheries claims, with consequent embarrassment to the Government.

The first indication in our own time that the Māori meant business over their Treaty claims to fisheries occurred in the Christchurch High Court in 1986. There, Judge Williamson overturned a conviction against Tom Te Weehi for taking undersize pāua. The case turned on section 88 (2) of the Fisheries Act 1983 which stated, 'Nothing in this Act shall affect any Māori fishing right.' Williamson ruled that Te Weehi was exercising a customary right to take shellfish for domestic consumption and section 88 exonerated him of other provisions in the Act.

The following year, the battle to reclaim the fisheries was joined in earnest when Judge Greig granted an injunction, sought by a coalition of tribes and the Māori Council, against the issue of Individual Transferable Quota for squid, jack mackerel and rock lobster. The case hinged on section 88 of the Fisheries Act, and advice from the Waitangi Tribunal that the sea was owned in the same way that land was. The sea was divided into zones controlled by tribes around the coastline. The court could find no evidence that Māori rights to the sea had been leased, alienated or extinguished. Furthermore, by issuing quota to companies and individual fishers, the Crown created a property right in the sea which it did not own. The court advised the Crown to negotiate with its Treaty partner for the use of their resource.

Māori negotiators claimed 100 percent ownership of the sea, but conceded a willingness to share 50 percent with their Treaty partner. The first Māori Fisheries Bill, designed to restore 50 percent of the quota to Māori ownership, met opposition from Fletcher Challenge. The Government withdrew the bill and replaced it with another. The Māori Fisheries Act 1989 returned only 10 percent of quota to Māori and established the Māori Fisheries Commission with a grant of $10 million to manage the quota under Aotearoa Fisheries. The Commission then launched Moana Pacific Fisheries, which purchased Fletcher Fishing for $20 million in a joint venture with Skeggs.

In the meantime, the question of ownership of the other 90 percent of quota remained unresolved. Māori could return to court at any time. The Minister of Justice, Doug Graham, did not relish that prospect. He warned his Cabinet colleagues that litigation was not the way to go because Māori had won ten cases in court against the Crown on their treaty rights. His solution of negotiating settlement of claims by meetings of 'chiefs with chiefs' culminated at the end of September in the signing of the agreement on the Sealord deal.

Under the agreement, the Government, would buy Māori a 50 percent stake in Sealord for $150 million. Māori would also receive 20 percent of quota on new species. In return, tribes signing the deal would relinquish the right to make any further commercial claims on fisheries. Only their customary rights to take shellfish for domestic use would remain intact. On first inspection, this attempt to settle the Māori fisheries claim looks good. Sealord holds 26 percent of quota, so Māori will ultimately end up with one-third of the fisheries. The snag is that the Sealord quota will remain in, and be fished by the company in a joint venture with, Brierley Investments. Not one job will be created where they are needed most in places like Northland and the East Coast, thus negating the purpose of the original claim. Instead, tribes will be allocated dividends from company profits for them to apply in job-creation projects. Not an easy task on the scrublands of Northland and the remote East Coast.

The Sealord deal, worked out between the Government and Māori negotiators, exemplifies the politics of expedience and pragmatism. The Government, according to the National Party manifesto, wants to settle all Māori Treaty grievances before the end of the decade. To this end, a global solution was needed. Sealord coming on to the market seemed ideal. Before the deal was signed, and immediately after, the Māori negotiators, like a mini-government, went round the tribes seeking their endorsement. They got a mixed reception of support and opposition. On the eve of signing, tribes were invited to the Beehive. In two hours, they were expected to digest a chunky document detailing the scheme, and put their signatures to this new treaty like their ancestors did in 1840. Tribes opposed to trading their aboriginal property rights to the sea for 150 pieces of silver have appealed to the Waitangi Tribunal.

1 March 1992
(*Metro*)

The Treaty of Wellington

THE DEED of Settlement between the Crown and Māori tribes over the Sealord deal has remarkable similarities to the Treaty of Waitangi. The deed purports to extinguish the commercial section of iwi property rights to the sea fisheries of New Zealand in exchange for the purchase of Sealord for $150 million. Because this deed replaces a section of the original Treaty, it is now being discussed in Māori circles as the 'Treaty of Wellington'.

The signing of this new treaty, like the original, was done in haste and poorly executed. The attempt at giving the document some semblance of legality by having signatures verified by Crown witnesses does not exculpate it from these strictures. When representatives of some tribes were invited to the Beehive to sign the deed, they were given an hour or so to read a twenty-six-page document, understand its economic, legal and political implications, and sign on behalf of their iwi. Their ancestors had more time than that. They had twenty-four hours to discuss a one-page document that was the Treaty of Waitangi. They would have had a further day had the missionaries not advanced the signing from the seventh to the sixth of February.

There is a total of ninety-three signatures on the Deed of Settlement, a long way short of the 540 collected on the original treaty. The method of signing was not consistent and systematic. At the top of the list are the names of the three Māori negotiators, Tīpene O'Regan, Matiu Rata, Sir Graham Latimer, and their three substitutes, Maanu Paul, Whata Winiata, and Richard Dargaville. There is no iwi designated beside these signatures, so their mandate to sign is as negotiators recognised by the Government. Six other signatures appear with no iwi beside them, two of them being the wives of the negotiators, Lady Latimer and Frances Winiata.

One signatory, Whata Winiata, signed the deed twice, as a Māori negotiator, and on behalf of the National Congress of Tribes. This parallels the Treaty of Waitangi, which Te Rauparaha signed twice. This new treaty goes one step further than the original by collecting the signature of two people three times. The first, Sir Graham Latimer, signed as a Māori negotiator, as a litigant in the Māori Fisheries Claim, and as President of the Māori Council. The second one signed on behalf of himself and two others who were not present.

The deed is between the Crown and iwi, but eighteen of the signatories appear under the designation Plaintiffs in the Fisheries Legislation. There is no iwi mandate beside their names. Others signed on behalf of waka (canoe confederations), trust boards, and rūnanga (multi-tribal councils). Two of the signatories are wrongly categorised as Māori negotiators.

There are twenty-one illegible signatures on the deed, which underlines the lack of precision in its execution. On some pages, there is a column where the full name of the person can be written legibly opposite the signature. Where this is lacking, one can only hazard a guess as to who the signatories were. One of the signatories, George Habib, is the administrative officer of the Māori negotiators. Beside his signature is the iwi Tūwharetoa, an inland tribe with no access to the sea. The lack of precision in the designation of iwi mandate beside so many signatures suggests that some of those present on the night of the signing got carried away by the hype of the occasion and signed with no mandate at all.

Given the flaws identified in the deed, it is not surprising that tribes not party to it came out in opposition. When the dissenting tribes lost an injunction against the deed in the High Court, Apirana Mahuika, chairman of the Tribal Congress, warned that the issue will come back to haunt the Government in future generations. It happened sooner than anticipated, and from unexpected quarters. Six Māori MPs from both sides of the House opposed the Sealords Settlement Bill when it was introduced into Parliament. John Carter, the junior government whip, and the backbencher Ross Meurant opposed a section of the bill reserving traditional seafood gathering areas for tribal use on the grounds that it was racist. The latter had to be mollified by amendments to the bill, ensuring wide consultation before reserves for Māori use were declared.

The ultimate embarrassment for the Government over the Sealord deal occurred in the world forum of the United Nations. Dr Tāmati Reedy, on behalf of the Tribal Congress, pleaded in the UN for an investigation into violations of indigenous rights by the Government's settlement of the Sealord deal. It is one of the ironies of history that Dr Reedy's Ngāti Porou ancestors fought on the side of the Crown against the Hauhau in the last century. In keeping with the conservative traditions of his people, Reedy stood aloof from Māori activism in the seventies and eighties. He worked for more than a decade as a subaltern within the bureaucratic system of Government. By keeping a low political profile, he rose to the top rank as Secretary of the Department of Māori Affairs. When it was disestablished in 1988, Reedy went into the lucrative business of consultancy work in the capital. By shopping the Government at the UN, Reedy has probably committed economic *hara kiri*. That is a measure of his now-passionate commitment to the Māori cause. The only conclusion to be drawn is that the Deed of Settlement, like the original treaty, has been botched by precipitate Crown action.

18 December 1992
(*Metro*)

Fighting over fish

THE SEALORD deal is causing ructions in the Māori world. Late in January, Te Puni Kōkiri, the Ministry of Māori Development, published a document, 'Māori Leadership and Decision Making'. The document was circulated widely among tribes to promote discussion on Māori leaders and the role they played as negotiators in the Sealord deal. Two of the Māori negotiators, Sir Graham Latimer and Tīpene O'Regan, took umbrage at the papers, and so did the Minister of Fisheries and Māori Affairs, Doug Kidd. Like their Pākehā counterparts, the corporate high-flyers in the commercial world, Latimer and O'Regan considered suing over comments about them in the papers. This method of silencing critics is alien to the open forum of the marae. It illustrates how much like Pākehā Māori have become at wheeling and dealing in power politics and the carve-up of resources.

Although the papers were primarily a critique of Māori leadership, the minister, Doug Kidd, was incensed at the view expressed that the Māori negotiators had surrendered the moral high ground of the Treaty of Waitangi for 150 pieces of silver. He was aggrieved that a Government-funded publication, put out by his own ministry, was critical of the Sealord deal. The minister suppressed any further distribution of the papers. So much for democracy. The minister's action served only to stimulate a demand for the papers and a spin-off for the photocopying industry.

At the heart of the discussion on leadership is the mandate of Māori negotiators and how they were validated to speak on behalf of the tribes in the fisheries negotiations with the Crown. Matiu Rata's platform to do so was Te Rūnanga o Muriwhenua, an incorporated council of the northernmost tribes of the Taitokerau district. Sir Graham Latimer derives his mandate as a Māori negotiator not from an iwi but from his role as president of the Māori Council. Because the council is a creature of Government, Sir Graham is characterised in the papers as having a subaltern role in maintaining the hegemony of the state. He had to negotiate a global settlement of the Māori fisheries claim that the Government could live with. Tīpene O'Regan operates as a Māori negotiator, with a tribal mandate from the Ngāi Tahu Trust Board and the Rūnanaga o Ngāi Tahu. But the Trust Board, too, is a creature of statute under the Ngāi Tahu Trust Board Act 1946. At least one of the South Island's tribes, Ngāi Poutini, holds dissenting views on O'Regan's role as a negotiator on their behalf.

Because of the strategic role they played in settling the Māori fisheries claim, Latimer was appointed chairman of Aotearoa Fisheries and O'Regan chairman of the Māori Fisheries Commission. The latter has subsequently been named chairman of the Sealord board as well. Ngāti Paoa, one of the tribes of the Hauraki Gulf, was aggrieved at the way these appointments were made without wider discussion among the people. Ngāti Paoa lodged a claim with the Waitangi Tribunal seeking a collective consultation with the tribes on appointments to the new Treaty of Waitangi Fisheries Commission.

Mr Kidd responded to a submission from the Waitangi Tribunal for wider consultations with iwi on appointments to the commission by calling a national hui at the Beehive in the middle of February. Prior to the meeting, the executive of the National Congress of Tribes met to prepare for the meeting. But instead of a unified position being laid down, a rift appeared in the congress. Ngāi Tahu decided to secede on a matter of principle. Charles Croft, chairman of the Ngāi Tahu Rūnanga, was critical of some of the working sub-committees of Congress accepting government funding for expenses incurred for consultation services. But there were other underlying reasons as well. Ngāi Tahu, as strong proponents of the Sealord deal, were aggrieved at Dr Tāmati Reedy criticising it at the United Nations and having his expenses paid by the Ministry of Māori Development. Although Reedy's trip was sanctioned by Congress chairman Apirana Mahuika, Croft argued there was no mandate for the trip from Ngāi Tahu.

An interesting aspect of these tribal contretemps is their

reflection of ancient tribal rivalries. Dr Reedy descends from Porourangi, the founding ancestor of Ngāti Porou. O'Regan and Croft descend from Tahu, the junior brother who cuckolded Porourangi and hived off to the South Island as a consequence of the scandal. In the past, it was a truism that 'Land and women were the reasons why men perished.' As one wit remarked, 'Fighting over fish is a comedown from women.'

Another contentious issue propounded by Tīpene O'Regan is the Ngāi Tahu claim to 70 percent of the fisheries on the basis of the more extended coastline of the South Island. The 200-mile Exclusive Economic Zone of the South Island incorporates the Chatham Islands and the sub-Antarctic waters of the Auckland Islands. The claim to the lucrative Chatham Island fishery is open to challenge by Moriori people, who have been given formal recognition by Government for the first time in the negotiations. The more populous tribes of the North Island argue that the benefits from the fisheries returned to Māori should be divided up on a population basis. These are thorny questions which the new commission will have to resolve. It will take a Solomon to sort out membership of the commission that would be acceptable to all tribes, especially when cupidity is already evident in the anticipated carve-up of dividends from a billion-dollar industry.

22 March 1993
(*Metro*)

Mana moana

THE GLOBAL settlement of the Māori fisheries claim by the Sealord deal was ill-conceived and flawed in principle. The flaw has become evident in the unseemly public fight over the division of spoils. The Ngāi Tahu of the South Island, led by Sir Tīpene O'Regan, argue on the basis of 'mana moana', that they should have 70 percent of the resource. This claim rests on the size of the fishery management areas of the South Island in New Zealand's

Exclusive Economic Zone. Besides the South Island's lengthy coastline, the zone incorporates both the Chatham and Auckland Islands. The importance of this zone, in terms of the Sealord settlement, is that the deal includes 10 percent of any new commercial species awaiting discovery and exploitation.

The more numerous northern tribes, on the other hand, led by Tu Wylie and Dick Dargaville, argue that the division of spoils should be based on population. In the protracted negotiations between 1987 and 1992 that culminated in the Sealord's Deed of Settlement, no forethought was given to the post-settlement phase beyond the establishment of the Māori Fisheries Commission.

If, at the outset of the fisheries claim, O'Regan had signalled his intention to claim 70 percent of the resources from Sealord, none of the tribes in the North Island would have signed. In any case, as things stood then, thirteen tribes rejected the Sealord deal. Sealord was a global settlement of tribal claims, whether they liked it or not. For this reason there should be a global distribution of the benefits.

Now, the division of spoils has been further complicated by urban Māori organisations wanting a piece of the action. Leading the charge is John Tamihere, executive officer of the Waipareira Trust in Auckland's western districts. Supporting the claim is MUMA, the Manukau Urban Māori Authority. Tamihere filed a claim with the Waitangi Tribunal, arguing that Māori serviced by the Trust are the modern equivalent of the tribes of the past. The chairman of the Māori Fisheries Commission, Sir Tīpene O'Regan, is so incensed that the tribunal agreed to a hearing that he is seeking a High Court ruling on the tribunal's jurisdiction in the matter. O'Regan argues that only tribes qualify for a share of Sealord, and if urban Māori want a share of its benefits, then they will have to reconnect with their tribes.

In pre-colonial times, the functioning political units of Māori society were hapū under individual chiefs, and iwi confederations under paramount chiefs. Hapū were the landholding units who sought to incorporate a stretch of the coastline in their territorial boundaries, some arable land for horticulture, and interior forest land for raw materials. Inland tribes staked out territories around lakeshores and river banks. The fundamental basis of tribal identity was ownership of land. Hapū, like micro-states, fought each other in defence of territory. Dispossessed tribes, ingested or absorbed by others, lost their identity. Consequently, tribes were not static entities. They were subject to the vagaries of fortune and the vicissitudes of war.

With the advent of Pākehā colonisation after 1840, the tribes were systematically dispossessed of their land by purchase, confiscation, and theft through legal artifice. By the turn of the century, the chiefs were disempowered by the loss of their mana whenua. By the second half of the twentieth century, only three million acres of Māori land remained of the sixty-six million they once owned *in toto*.

With a burgeoning population on an inadequate land-base, life in tribal polities was no longer tenable. In the postwar years, the urban migration and diaspora followed. The abandonment of tribalism was actively encouraged by the Government's urban relocation programme.

The contemporary reality of Māori is that 80 percent live outside their tribal areas in towns and cities within New Zealand and across the Tasman. Māori enclaves can even be found in London, Vancouver, and Salt Lake City. For them, tribalism remains only as an ideology, which is sustained by periodic visits to home marae. There, where endemic unemployment may be as high as 50 percent, and even 70 percent in some places, tribalism is artificially sustained by Government-initiated trust boards and social welfare programmes. Tribes as entities become manifest only occasionally at meetings of trust boards, rūnanga and hui for *rites de passage* such as tangi, weddings and birthdays. The only tūrangawaewae (standing place) of tribes today are 500 or so marae reserves around the country. But no one lives on them any more in the communal manner of the past, except for marae with pensioner housing. The latter are usually found on urban marae established by quasi-tribes that emerged out of the diaspora.

The transformation of tribalism by the abandonment of

papakāinga saw the emergence of quasi-tribes in the form of urban Māori organisations. These voluntary associations are a mix of tribal, religious and secular groups for the purposes of mutual support and cultural maintenance, functions once carried out by the tribe. New metropolitan and parochial identities were forged as Ngāti Pōneke (Wellington tribe), Ngāti Ākarana (Auckland tribe) and Ngāti Ōtara.

When a critical density of Māori population was reached in different suburbs, new groups emerged around culture clubs, Māori sections of orthodox churches, Māori committees, and Women's Welfare League and marae committees. The symbolic embodiment of these new group identities are urban marae. Their multitribal underpinnings are symbolised by names such as Te Ūnga Waka (landing place of canoes), Ngā Hau e Whā (The Four Winds), and Tātai Hono (conjoined lines of descent).

With the advent of PEP and TOPs employment programmes, the quasi-tribes of urban marae became delivery and service mechanisms for the Government. The Hone Waititi Marae in west Auckland became such a large provider of education, training, welfare and employment services that it had to corporatise itself as the Waipareira Trust. Waipareira Corporate Services is the urban equivalent of a tribal trust board. As the new kid on the block, Tamihere is more than justified in telling Sir Tīpene to move over. In the past, the true rangatira did, by making space for refugees. The ball is in Sir Tīpene's court.

25 July 1995
(*Metro*)

6: OPENING THE FISCAL ENVELOPE

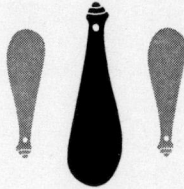

Direct negotiation and the fiscal envelope

NEW ZEALAND is one of the few countries in the world where a nation state was brought into being by social contract between indigenous people and an imperial power. That contract, known as the Treaty of Waitangi, enabled the British Crown, in the person of the Governor, to establish kāwanatanga, a system of government in the land. In return, the Crown guaranteed the continued existence of chiefly power. What the chiefs did not understand in the nineteenth century was the nature of the Crown as a legal fiction. Foucault asserts that sovereignty, in the form of the Crown, is one of the great inventions of bourgeois society. He states:

> The theory of sovereignty, and the organisation of the legal code centred upon it, have allowed the system of right to be superimposed upon the mechanisms of discipline in such a way as to conceal its procedures, the element of domination inherent in its techniques, and to guarantee to everyone, the exercise of his proper sovereign rights by virtue of the state.[1]

The fiction fostered by the purveyors of the Treaty was the ideology of the Crown as a benevolent, all-powerful monarch guaranteeing Māori rights. The ideology masked the reality of power being vested in Parliament, which was not bound by the Treaty.

Once the Treaty was signed, the Governor and his successors laid down the foundations of the state, consisting of a centralised administration, legal system, judiciary, and military power. Kāwanatanga was clearly something greater than the single personality of the Governor. It eventually evolved into Parliament, and the machinery of the state. The state, with its monopoly on power to coerce obedience to law and its designs for Māori, had an inherent potential to use that force to dominate and oppress.

History is littered with broken treaties, and the Treaty of Waitangi is no exception. Colonial despoliation followed as Parliament stripped Māori of their land and fisheries by military invasion, confiscation and legal artifice. Māori, on the other hand, were not passive victims. They resorted to armed struggle, passive resistance, inter-tribal discourse, and the formation of two pan-tribal councils to make submissions to Parliament.

Eventually, the modernist project which justified colonialism ran its course. In the post-modern era of urbanisation, the counter-narrative promoted by radical Māori politics emerged. The subjugated discourses of the tribes were aired in the forum of the Waitangi Tribunal, and the mass media of the Fourth Estate. The empowerment of the Waitangi Tribunal to examine Māori land grievances retrospective to 1840 opened up the past for interrogation. Both Labour and National governments had to deal with the past in an electoral climate that grew increasingly hostile to the seemingly endless Māori claims. Within this historic framework sits the Crown's agenda of 'direct negotiation' and the so-called 'fiscal envelope'.

The National Government's policy of settling Māori treaty claims by direct negotiation within a fiscal envelope, and a timeframe of the year 2000, is a negation of tino rangatiratanga and the promise of partnership under the Treaty of Waitangi. Without the evidence adduced by tribunal hearings, attendant publicity in the media, and the

A Christmas card goes a long way.

Christmas Mailing Dates:

For International Express, Air and Economy services, send your mail by the following dates:

Destination	Economy	Air	Express
Australia (zone A)	Monday 19 November	Friday 14 December	Tuesday 18 December
South Pacific (zone B)	Monday 12 November	Monday 10 December	Tuesday 18 December
East Asia & North America (zone C)	Monday 12 November	Monday 10 December*	Tuesday 18 December
UK & Europe (zone D)	Monday 12 November	Monday 10 December	Tuesday 18 December
Rest of the World (zone E)	Monday 12 November	Friday 7 December	Tuesday 18 December

* This date applies to parcels and letters to East Asia and letters to North America. Parcels to North America should be mailed by Monday 3rd December.

Christmas mailing dates are published as a guide only. New Zealand Post makes every effort to deliver Christmas mail in time for Christmas, but can't guarantee delivery.

Compensation for loss or damage up to NZ$2,000 (Express) and NZ$250 (Air and Economy) is included with the option to purchase additional cover up to NZ$50,000 (Express) and NZ$1,500 (Air and Economy).

For more information on international services, please contact our Customer Service Centre on **0800 501 501** (Monday - Friday, 7.30am - 7pm; Saturday, 9am - 1pm) or visit **www.nzpost.com**

New Zealand Post

moral weight of tribunal recommendations, Māori negotiators engage in direct negotiations with the Crown from a
position of disempowerment.

The strategy of settling Treaty claims by direct negotiation has its genesis in the Treaty policies of the Fourth Labour
Government. Labour had been so long in the political
wilderness that it had no institutional memory of the role of
the state as a mechanism of colonial domination. With a
threat looming to its forty-year tenure of the Māori seats
from Mana Motuhake and radical Māori politics, Labour felt
the need to do something substantive for its Māori constituents. Flush from its Bastille Day victory in the snap
election of 1984, the Government introduced the bill to make
the Waitangi Tribunal retrospective to 1840. Although the
bill languished for a year on the agenda of the House, it
eventually became law as the Treaty of Waitangi Amendment Act 1985. Its successful passage through the final
reading in the House was managed by placing it near the
end of a crowded agenda before the House rose for
Christmas.

The effect of retrospective empowerment of the Tribunal
was immediate, as upwards of 150 claims were filed in 1986.
Overwhelmed by claims, the three-man Tribunal was also
paralysed when a member became ill. Over the next twelve
months, the Tribunal was increased to seven and eventually
sixteen members to enable it to increase the number of
sittings. Its research capacity was also strengthened.[2]

Labour's treaty policy leading up to the 1990 election
was marked by the inscription of the Treaty in a number of
statutes, including the Criminal Justice Act 1985, the Law
Commission Act 1985, the Environment Act 1986, the State
Owned Enterprises Act 1986, the Māori Language Act 1987,
the Conservation Act 1987, the State Sector Act 1988, the
Coroner's Act 1988, the Treaty of Waitangi Amendment Act
1988, the Treaty of Waitangi (State Enterprises) Act 1988,
the Māori Affairs Restructuring Act 1989, the Māori Fisheries
Act 1989, the Crown Forests Act 1989, the Children, Young
Persons and their Families Act 1989, and the Education Act
1989.

Inscription of the Treaty in legislation was not confined to Labour. The process began under the National Government with the Fisheries Amendment Act 1983. The inclusion in section 88 (2) 'that nothing in this act shall contradict Māori fishing rights' revived a long-forgotten provision in the 1877 Fisheries Act. It was included at the behest of the Māori Council. The fact that this provision had not been repealed and had been dormant for more than a century probably seduced the Government into seeing it as a benign clause that would have little effect on its management of the political economy.

When National resumed the Treasury benches in 1990, it continued the trend, expanded on by Labour, of inscribing the Treaty in legislation, with the Resource Management Act 1991, the Crown Minerals Act 1991, and the Treaty of Waitangi Fisheries Claims Settlement Act 1992.

The wide-ranging inscription of references to rights under the Treaty of Waitangi in twenty-three statutes elevated the treaty to the level of a constitutional instrument. Māori responded by challenging the actions of the Crown in the High Court. The first success came in the High Court at Christchurch in 1986. Justice Williamson overturned a conviction in the District Court against Tom Te Weehi for taking undersized pāua on the grounds that he was exercising a customary fishing right to take shellfish for domestic consumption.

Thereafter, the role of the Crown in the control and allocation of resources was challenged by organised Māori interests, including tribal rūnanga, trust boards and the Māori Council. In 1987, successful actions against the Crown included injunctions against the ITQ fisheries management regime, the State Owned Enterprises Act, and the Huakina Trust against the Waikato Valley Authority. In 1989, the Tainui Trust Board successfully fought the sale of Coalcorp, and the Māori Council the sale of forest assets. In 1991, Te Rūnunga o Muriwhenua succeeded in its fight over fisheries, as did the Māori Council over the sale of radio frequencies and in seeking protection of Māori interest in broadcasting.

The watershed in the Māori struggle to recover assets

from the state was marked by the successful injunctions in 1987 against the State Owned Enterprises Act and the ITQ fisheries management regime. In the SOE case, Justice Cooke ruled that the inclusion of the principles of the Treaty in section 9 of the SOE Act had the effect of a constitutional guarantee within the field covered by the Act. In relation to land held by the Crown, he said never again would it be possible to put aside a Māori land grievance. Justice Bisson reinforced that conclusion with the statement that the advent of legislation invoking the principles of the Treaty meant that the Treaty could no longer be treated as 'a simple nullity'.[3] The judgement slowed down the transfer of Crown land to SOEs until adequate safeguards for Māori land claims under the Treaty of Waitangi were put in place.

The Māori fisheries claim against the Government's ITQ system had an even greater impact on the management of the political economy than the SOE claim. Justice Greig ruled that the quota system breached Māori fishing rights guaranteed under section 88 (2) of the Fisheries Act and put an interim stop to the system until the existence or otherwise of Māori fishing rights was resolved.

Māori negotiators claimed 100 percent ownership of the fisheries but expressed a willingness to concede a 50 percent share to its Treaty partner. The Crown could not disprove the claim because, unlike the land, the Crown had no deeds of sale over the sea, or any documents eliminating Māori customary rights to fisheries in favour of the Crown.

Even the modest claim of 50 percent threatened vested interests and the stability of the fishing industry. The state, as the critical theorists averred, was moved to contain and eventually try to eliminate this risk to the system.[4] As an interim measure, the Crown returned 10 percent of quota to Māori and a payment of $10 million under the management of the Māori Fisheries Commission. The Māori Fisheries Act 1989 ensured that the Commission was integrated into the political economy without causing undue dysfunction to the system. In the meantime, the Māori negotiators of the fisheries claim continued talks with the Crown over the remaining 40 percent of their claim.

The potential of Māori land and fishery claims to destabilise the political economy impelled the Government to establish the Treaty of Waitangi Policy Unit in 1988. TOWPU assumed the lead role in the Task Force for co-ordinating the Crown's position for hearings of the Waitangi Tribunal. TOWPU was also responsible for establishing procedures for the conduct of direct negotiations in the settlement of claims between the Crown and claimants.

In the three-year lead-up to the 1990 elections, National in Opposition mounted a vigorous attack on Labour's Treaty policy. The Government reacted in 1988 by promulgating the 'Principles for Crown Action on the Treaty of Waitangi'. This document signalled the supremacy of the Crown by declaring the ascendancy of the principle of kāwanatanga over rangatiratanga. The principle of rangatiratanga was diminished to one of self-management. This redefinition of the relationship between the Crown and its Treaty partner was an assertion of government control and a public renunciation of Labour's Treaty policy. It was to no avail. Labour lost the election.

It took a year for the National Government to come to grips with Māori treaty claims. In a Memorandum to the Cabinet Strategy Committee dated 17 March 1992, the Minister of Justice, Doug Graham, put forward his proposals. He argued that the inscription of the Treaty in 23 statutes could not now be easily reversed. The Crown had suffered ten embarrassing losses in litigating Māori claims in the High Court. Litigation held up the business of government and was unnecessarily costly to both Crown and claimants. Therefore, the minister argued, it was better to avoid litigation where claims were well founded and enter into direct negotiations with the claimants. Direct negotiation meant 'chiefs meeting with chiefs'. Although this proposal implied a meeting of equals, it was far from that. On the Crown's side, the Minister of Justice would be supported by an 'A team' of chief executives and top officials and the resources of the state. On the Māori side would be claimants with no substantive land base, limited financial resources and little experience of dealing with the Crown.

The minister also reminded Cabinet that the election manifesto of the National Party aimed to settle all Treaty claims by the year 2000. He warned that in attempting to achieve settlement in that timeframe, the Government's cheque-book was not limitless. This was the first intimation of a fiscal cap for the settlement of claims.

In the meantime, Māori negotiators continued talks with the Crown on the residual 40 percent of the Māori fisheries claim. When Carter Holt signalled the sale of Sealord for $375 million, the negotiators struck a deal with the Crown. Under the Deed of Settlement, signed at Parliament in September 1992, the Government agreed to purchase for Māori a $150 million half-share of Sealord in a joint venture with Brierley Investments. With the deal went 50 percent of quota on all new species.

In exchange for the Sealord deal, the Māori negotiators agreed to a clause in the deed to repeal section 88 (2) of the Fisheries Act 1983, thereby eliminating a Treaty right to make any further commercial claims to fisheries.[5] Equally as invidious was a clause acknowledging the Treaty of Waitangi Settlement Fund.[6] Under this clause the negotiators recognised that:

> The Crown has fiscal constraints and that this settlement will necessarily restrict the Crown's ability to meet from any fund which the Crown establishes as part of the Crown's overall settlement framework, the settlement of other claims arising from the Treaty of Waitangi.

Despite opposition in the House and the High Court, the model of a global settlement of the Māori Fisheries claim set a precedent for the possible settlement of all land claims by the year 2000. Behind the scenes, the Crown and Māori negotiators discussed their options. Bancorp acted as financial advisors. In 1994, a solution was arrived at and unveiled by the Prime Minister in January.

The plan was predicated on a fiscal cap of an unstated amount, complemented by the inclusion of key resources. A Waitangi Commission would be established to administer the settlement on behalf of claimants, with 10 percent of the settlement consisting of cash and land of spiritual value. Key resources such as Forestcorp, Landcorp, Coalcorp, Electricorp and, of course, Sealord would make up 90 percent. The value of these assets amounts to $1 billion, the rumoured level of the fiscal cap.

When the fiscal envelope was aired in May on the *Frontline* television programme, Māori activists came out in opposition after a decade of quiescence. Leading the charge was Te Kawau Maro, a pan-tribal student group at Auckland University and AIT. Te Kawau Maro targeted Māori negotiators as 'sellouts', organised a large meeting in Tānenuiarangi in opposition to the envelope and mounted demonstrations outside the High Court.

Te Kawāriki, an activist group in Northland, also came out in opposition. The Taumata Kaumātue of Taitokerau expressed their opposition by seeking an injunction against the fiscal envelope.

In the capital city, the Māori Legal Services sought disclosure of information with a complaint to the Ombudsman.

The return to activism was not without effect. The Government Treaty Policy Unit decided to reject the Sealord model of the pan-Māori approach in the settlement of claims and draw up a new set of guidelines for Treaty claims.

3 October 1994
(Seminar, Māori Studies Department, University of Auckland)

Roundly rejected

IN DECEMBER, the Government invited a select group of Māori leaders to the Beehive to launch the Crown Proposals for the Settlement of Treaty Claims. The original draft document was leaked in November and circulated widely among Māori people, including radical activists. The controversy surrounding that document, and the concept of a fiscal envelope for the settlement of Māori land claims, made the public launch of the official document highly political. Activists staged a theatrical burning of the document in front of the Minister of Justice on the steps of Parliament. For this reason, Sir Hepi Te Heuheu and Dame Te Atairangikaahu declined to attend the ceremony at the Beehive. Ariki, like the British royals, have to be above the rough and tumble of politics.

When the National Government came to power in 1990, it took a whole year to come to grips with Māori Treaty claims. Leading up to the election, National in Opposition vehemently opposed the Labour Government's Treaty policy. Jim Bolger claimed that the findings of the Tribunal were 'gnawing' at the hearts of (Pākehā) New Zealanders. The Waitangi Tribunal was even accused of being racially biased because there was only one Pākehā member and two Māori members. Curiously this charge was not levelled at the inception of the Tribunal when it was the other way around. It was no more than a cheap political shot. But once in power, it was a different matter. The National Government had to come to grips with the reality of Māori land claims, the Treaty, and the Tribunal.

In 1992, the Minister of Justice, Doug Graham, reminded Cabinet of National's election manifesto promise to settle all Treaty claims by the year 2000. Although it was a rash promise, given the extent of the colonial rip-off of Māori as exemplified by the 400 claims before the Tribunal, he felt obliged to deliver on the promise.

Fortunately for the minister, the previous Government had put in place the Treaty of Waitangi Policy Unit. The unit, known as TOWPU, was put to work to generate policy to meet the Government's objectives. Unfortunately, the exercise lapsed back to the centralised-control mode of unilateral decision-making. The discourse of equality and Treaty partnership evaporated. It was not yet fixed as part of institutional memory. The lack of Māori consultation prejudiced the policy at the outset.

The Treaty settlement proposals sets out a government framework for the negotiation and settlement of Māori grievances in a quest for justice which hitherto had no rules. The first principle in the framework is acknowledgement of historic injustice by the Crown where the evidence is well founded. When the matter was debated in the House, it was a quantum leap forward to hear the Prime Minister, Jim Bolger, acknowledge that the Crown had perpetrated injustice against Māori. Although the present generation of Pākehā were not culpable, they did have a responsibility to put things right.

However, in attempting to resolve injustice, the Crown would follow the principle of not doing so if it meant creating further injustice, such as returning private land to Māori ownership. Although reassuring to present landholders, it offered cold comfort to Māori whose land was taken and given to Pākehā settlers. Less reassuring is the assertion of the principle of majority rule – that the Crown's duty is to act in the best interests of all New Zealanders. It was this very principle that reduced Māori to a minority in their own land and subjected them to the 'tyranny of the majority', that Alexis de Tocqueville identified as the flaw in democracy.

One of the problems bedevilling the Government in dealing with Māori is the clamour of voices wanting to be heard. Who among them have the right to speak on behalf of the tribes? In the last century the Crown itself undermined the authority of chiefs and their iwi by the expropriation of their resources. The result in our time is the multiple discourses of claim and counter-claim from trust boards, rūnanga, incorporations, individuals, and ad hoc groups.

The Labour Government tried to rationalise the situation with its Rūnanga-a-Iwi Act but it was thrown out by Winston Peters when National came to power. Now the attempt to establish a system of mandating Māori negotiators is being revisited in the policy document.

The first step is an amendment to the Treaty of Waitangi Act enabling the Tribunal to decline to hear claims not lodged and mandated by iwi or hapū. Negotiators will be required to have a deed of mandate from their iwi or hapū to be recognised by the Government. This is a tall order considering the diaspora of iwi and hapū since the Second World War.

The claimant group also has to have a structure of

governance in place ready to receive and manage proceeds from settlements. In past settlements, the Crown established statutory trust boards for the purpose. This time round it seems the tribes have the right to devise the structure of governance for themselves. This is a welcome step forward, which will enable tribes to be more enterprising in the marketplace in the investment of their funds.

While the framework proposals seem rational and reasonable, their acceptance by Māori is prejudiced by the last principle in the document – a fiscal envelope setting a cap of $1 billion on the Crown's ability to make reparations. In the timeframe of settling claims by the year 2000, the Government is also trying to reduce overseas debt by $17 billion. It is a coincidence that this figure almost matches the internal debt to Māori of the major raupatu (confiscation claims) amounting to $18 billion.

The current price of dairy land ranges from $5,000–$10,000 an acre. The $18 billion compensation for three million acres of raupatu land is arrived at by taking the current value of dairy land at the lower end of the scale. In view of the disparity between what the Government is paying its overseas creditors and what it is offering on its internal debt, it is predictable that the fiscal envelope will be roundly rejected by the tribes.

26 January 1995
(*Metro*)

Masters of theatre

IT HAS BEEN almost two decades since New Zealand's senior anthropologist, Dame Joan Metge, wrote a paper entitled, 'Talking past each other'. At that time, the modern discourse of radical Māori politics was gathering momentum. Metge was concerned that the messages coming from one cultural frame of reference to another were not being properly decoded across the cultural divide. Consequently, protagonists in cultural politics between Māori and Pākehā ended up 'talking past each other'. Events in the last month seem to indicate that nothing much has changed. Indeed, it appears that the Government is even more obtuse than its predecessors of twenty years ago.

Late in January, a hui of over a thousand responsible Māori leaders convened at Tūrangi by Sir Hepi Te Heuheu rejected the fiscal envelope of a billion dollars to settle all Māori treaty claims. At that hui, Māori luminaries including Sir Paul Reeves, Bishop Bennett, Professor Mason Durie, and Professor Syd Mead made common cause with activists Mike Smith, Hone Harawira and others in rejecting the fiscal envelope.

Unfortunately, the Minister of Justice, Doug Graham, missed a cue to back off from the envelope. Instead, he condemned the hui as premature and uninformed. The minister's comment on the hui was well astray in view of the discussion over six months on the leaked Treaty settlement policy papers leading up to Tūrangi. In fact, there had been an earlier hui in November at Ōmarumutu Marae in Ōpōtiki designed to generate a unified response to Treaty settlement proposals among tribes who had suffered raupatu (land confiscation) at the hands of the Crown. The tribes involved included Whakatōhea, Ngāti Awa, Tūhoe and Ngāiterangi from the Bay of Plenty, Tainui from the Waikato, and Āti Awa from Taranaki. The build-up of Māori opinion, as it has been historically against Crown policies, was slow, considered and deliberate.

Doug Graham's dismissal of the Tūrangi hui, combined with his determination to press ahead with twelve regional hui sponsored by the Government to discuss the Crown's settlement policies, set the stage for the events at Waitangi. By pressing ahead with its plan of action, the Government gave the activists *carte blanche* to deliver the message against the fiscal envelope a second time in a more vehement manner, accompanied by the full range of Māori oratory, rhetoric, and symbolic gestures.

Māori are masters of theatre, and the marae is the stage where orators strut their stuff in the cut and thrust of debate. In the past it was not uncommon to 'raise the dust' on the marae with vigorous body language. When feelings ran high, arguments were occasionally settled by bruising physical contact, hence the courtyard in front of the ancestral house was also known as 'the marae of Tūmatauenga', the god of war. When there is tension and conflict between groups, the marae is as much a bear-pit as Parliament, as it has been characterised by Jim Anderton.

So when Government ministers go to marae, as they did at Waitangi, they can expect a rough time, to be called to account by the people. Theatrical gestures, the prancing haka, baring buttocks, spitting on the ground, stomping on a flag, are ritual gestures of defiance against the power of government. These actions are in keeping with the burning of the policy document on the steps of Parliament, the chainsaw attack on One Tree Hill, and the decapitation of the statue of John Ballance at Wanganui. The Government should not be surprised when these latter-day Hōne Heke do their thing to communicate unequivocally Māori opposition to a policy that is seen to be arbitrary, unilaterally defined, and a denial of justice. Only the spitting on the Governor-General cast a discordant note. Although discomfiting for Her Excellency Dame Catherine, in a perverse way it was a recognition of her status. No one spits on commoners.

Despite the vehemence of the opposition to the fiscal envelope at Waitangi, the Government went ahead doggedly with its regional hui, thereby going from one embarrassment to the next. At Rotorua, the Arawa set up three checkpoints en route to the marae to defuse any potential for trouble. Although the decorum of the occasion was maintained, the Government was nonetheless humiliated by a symbolic display of mana Māori. When the ariki Sir Hepi Te Heuheu arrived after the ministers of the Crown, he was accorded a standing welcome. Mana ariki had its moment of triumph over the temporal mana of the Crown.

At the hui in Ōpōtiki, the veteran protester Tame Iti, nowadays adorned with a full facial moko, outdid his actions at Waitangi. He went on to the Terere Marae equipped with a step-ladder. In a symbolic gesture of mana, Tame Iti ascended the latter to speak from a lofty height.

The Crown officials had to look up to him as he berated the Government over the fiscal envelope.

At Huria Marae, in Tauranga, the ministers were accorded the honour of a wero, the ritual challenge by a warrior skilled in the weaponry of the taiaha. But it was a challenge with a difference as he threw down the rolled-up document of the fiscal envelope, instead of a dart, and stomped on it.

At the fifth hui in Te Kuiti, the fiscal envelope was shredded in front of the Prime Minister, Mr Bolger, and his Government accused of being trustees for thieves. One speaker advocated that the Government's actions over the fiscal envelope should be subjected to adjudication by the International Court of Justice.

Is Māori discourse being ignored, or has it, as Metge has suggested, been misunderstood? The media construction of the events at Waitangi Marae on 6 February as a 'disgrace', a day of 'bitter confrontation' and a 'shattered ceremony' gave the impression of an irreconcilable gulf between Māori and Pākehā. That impression was also engendered by the Government's overreaction of cancelling the evening commemoration ceremony of the 155th anniversary of the signing of the Treaty of Waitangi. Ten days later, Prime Minister Bolger announced the end of Waitangi Day and the possible return of the name to New Zealand Day. It was a strange reaction to cancel one historic hui while brazening out twelve others.

28 February 1995
(*Metro*)

7: TWO WORLDS

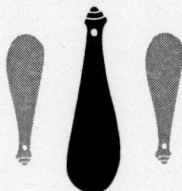

Billy T.'s tangi

THE CLASH between two cultures last month over the funeral arrangements for the late Billy T. James brought the cultural divide between Māori and Pākehā out into the public arena. The divide for too long has been denied by the prevailing Pākehā ideology of one people. Māori have tried to counter that ideology with their own one of biculturalism, meaning two people in one nation.

The agenda of biculturalism is both social and political. At the social level it means understanding the values and norms of the other culture and being able to fit in comfortably when an occasion demands. At the political level, biculturalism means power-sharing in the decision-making processes of the country. The charter for power-sharing is the Treaty of Waitangi, signed on behalf of Pākehā by Governor Hobson and the chiefs of New Zealand for their Māori descendants.

Pākehā outrage over the Tainui takeover of the funeral arrangements for one of New Zealand's most gifted entertainers indicates how monocultural most New Zealanders still are after 150 years of Māori and Pākehā living together. If Pākehā were as bicultural as most Māori are, they would not have asked on the *Holmes* show what gave the Māori people the right to decide the fate of Mr James's body.

Humans have two complementary components to their personality as individuals and social beings. Each individual born into the world is genetically unique. That uniqueness is the basis of their individuality. But no individual, such as Billy T. James, however unique his talent, is an island unto himself. James was born into a whānau, an extended family of up to twenty or thirty members. Within that whānau were mutual obligations for loving, nurturing and caring. The whānau in its turn is embedded in the wider kin group of the hapū, the sub-tribe, which may number up to several hundred people. The hapū is in turn part of a wider kin group known as the iwi.

In the case of Billy T., he belonged to the Tainui Confederation of tribes, whose members number over 120,000 people. These groups, in ascending order of precedence, have first claim over an individual. In Māori lore, non-kin, including Māori and Pākehā, have no claim at all. Pākehā who enter into cross-cultural marriages need to know what is likely to happen in the event of the decease of their spouse.

On the occasion of bereavement, the whānau, known as the kirimate, are enfolded and protected by the hapū. The latter takes over all the responsibilities of making the arrangements for the tangi. This includes notifying friends and kin, preparing the marae, manning the paepae with orators night and day, feeding the guests for the duration of the tangi, arranging for the undertaker, the church service, the digging of the grave and the hākari (funerary feast). Should the deceased be affiliated to several hapū, then other hapū will contest the right to be in charge. The more important the person, the greater the contest. The hapū which makes the strongest case in terms of whakapapa (genealogy) and traditions usually wins. But often a compromise is reached with stopovers at marae of other hapū.

The tangi and its rituals fulfil basic social functions. Firstly, the bereaved are enfolded by the gift of love from kin and friends in their hour of grief. Secondly, the tangi is a form of catharsis, which, by its nature, facilitates the grieving process. The kirimate, as the chief mourners, keep the death watch beside the deceased night and day. As each group of visitors arrive to pay their respects, they evoke an upwelling of emotions in the bereaved so that there is a liberal flow of mucus and tears. The process goes on twenty-four hours of the day for the duration of the tangi. By the time of the burial, the chief mourners are emotionally drained and death requited by their tears. The hākari follows as the public send-off to the deceased.

For the kirimate, there is one further ritual which is usually conducted by their closest kin. This is the takahi whare (tramping the house) ceremony. A minister lifts the tapu on the house and exhorts the spirit of the deceased to depart to the realm of the spirit world. Then follows the pō whakamoe, the night bringing sleep and rest. Some people may stay on with the kirimate for several days to help reintegrate them back into the world of the living.

Some Pākehā have been affronted by the Tainui assertion of their right to conduct the tangi for Billy T. in the manner described above. Although it was none of their business, they made much of the wishes of James and his wife for a church service, followed by burial on Taupiri Mountain. As the Tainui elders pointed out, there was no way the latter wish could have been met without lying in state on the marae. Although Billy T. was a national figure, he was essentially a humble man. He would not have presumed to lie in state on the Queen's marae as a right. That was an honour for his people to bestow on him, which they did in full measure. It was the only way that the thousands of people who went to pay tribute to Billy T. could have been accommodated. On this occasion, Māori custom prevailed over the wishes of the widow because Billy T. was Māori and he belonged to Tainui. The media hype about the event by ignorant, monocultural commentators only served to inflame the situation between Māori and Pākehā.

Throughout the tangi, Tainui extended the olive branch to Mrs James. Although she personally did not respond to the invitation, she did send an emissary to bring back her daughter. Therein lies room for cultural reconciliation in the future, when the mortuary rituals for Billy T. are completed by the unveiling of his headstone.

No reira e te tohunga whakangahau, hoki atu ki tō ūkaipō. Haere ki Hawaiki nui, ki Hawaiki roa, ki Hawaiki pāmamao, ki te Hono i wairua.

Therefore to you, master entertainer, return to the bosom which nurtured you in the night. Farewell, go to great Hawaiki, distant Hawaiki, far Hawaiki, to the gathering place of spirits.

12 August 1991
(*Listener*)

Community justice?

Letter from Mt Eden Prison
Jah Rastafari
14 July 1989

Justice lives, man shall not live on bread alone, but by every word and action that proceedeth from him. I and others are moved to take up this cross of fasting as an endeavour that the Māori people have the right to be heard before the elders on their own marae. Repatriation is a must for us to survive in this soul-destroying system. Labourers are needed to push for the right of judgement in our own household first, that is on our own marae. Equally we are prepared for change, shown through this deed (fasting), from the old, unbalanced human standards of the Crown court, to a council of kaumātua who are aware and able to provide the spiritual need or direction of physical labour for offenders who have lost their Māori direction. This unity has to be implemented for the survival of our Māoritanga and wairuatanga and that our children will not have to suffer insurrection in these jails, and Pākehā law standards. An announcement was made in the Mt Eden chapel on 12 July 1989 of the commencement of peaceful resistance by fasting. We shall continue this push until higher powers recognise that the jails are evil and the law is oppressive to Māori spirituality. Let righteousness cover the earth like water covers the sea.

John Heeney
G. Terekia
T. Joyce

The men who signed this letter sent me a copy per medium of a third person, requesting that their fast, and the reasons underlying it, be brought to the attention of the public. The letter ends with two profound thoughts. Jails are evil, and the law is oppressive. Both need to be transformed, so that righteousness prevails. Their remedy for the problems that beset them in a monocultural system of law and justice is to be judged in their own house on the marae under the jurisdiction of kaumātua.

This demand for Māori autonomy in the administration of justice is just another facet of the Māori renaissance which has gathered momentum in this decade. The demand has been condemned as separatist, and will not be countenanced by the Minister of Justice, Mr Palmer. The minister's reaction of staking out a rigidly conservative position is unfortunate. By digging in the way he has, Mr Palmer closes off options posed by the radical potential of Māori to transform a judicial system which has failed to deal constructively with their needs.

Judges, lawyers and superintendents of penal institutions know that courts and prisons are a failure. They do not deter criminal behaviour, nor do they reform criminals. Yet they take no steps to reform the system, because it is what society wants. Penal institutions fulfil a deeply rooted, primitive need in humans for revenge and punishment of offenders. In other words, courts simply provide a civilised veneer for utu. But utu is a two-way process. When the offender is released at the end of his sentence, he exacts utu by offending again. Being a judge in a criminal court dealing with recidivists must be one of the most disheartening professions in life.

The pattern of Māori reoffending begins with youths of 14–16 years of age sentenced to borstal training. Within the first year of release, 61 percent reoffend. Within four years, 90 percent reoffend. By their seventeenth birthday, 40 percent of Māori youth would have had at least one court appearance compared to 10 percent for Pākehā. This pattern of reoffending is repeated into adult life by young men who appear before the courts on criminal charges. It is not until the age of thirty that the pattern changes and offending stops.

The reason for this dismal state of affairs is because the judicial system is alien to the lives and reality of young Māori. Offenders are usually apprehended by white policemen, defended by white lawyers on legal aid, in a situation they do not comprehend. In court their sense of alienation is exacerbated when they are addressed by white court officials who mispronounce their names, and judged, admonished and sentenced by a white judge they do not know or even respect. The whole judicial process is a strange, dehumanising experience, where the offender does not speak for himself, has no whānau in support, and has to have his case put to the judge by a third person. The court symbolises the powerlessness of Māori people to control their own lives. It is not until they get to prison that any semblance of normalcy returns. There offenders are among their peers, where 50 percent of the inmates are brown. Paremoremo Maximum Security Prison holds no fear for Māori offenders. The hidden curriculum teaches them the tricks of the trade so they can do better jobs when they get outside.

The cost of running a judicial and penal system which does not work is astronomical. For instance, the Ōtara machete murder trial cost $870,522 in legal aid. The Harawira trial and appeal cost $79,600. The recent Mongrel Mob trial cost over $1 million. In 1988, legal aid cost the taxpayer $30 million. When a conviction is obtained, the cost of feeding and lodging an offender while detaining him or her at Her Majesty's pleasure has to be added to the initial costs of legal aid. Those costs do not take into account the salaries of police, probation officers, court officials, administrators and judges. The question needs to be asked, is society prepared to continue paying these costs to satisfy the desire for retribution, or is there an alternative? It is a moot point as to who is paying the most for utu between society and Māori offenders. Māori people suggest there is a way out, through a Māori system of justice. The Hui Taumata, the Māori Economic Development Conference 1984, called for an end to 'negative funding' such as the expenditure on prisons. Instead, it advocated diversion of funds saved towards positive community development, such as Māori adjudication, management, control and reformation of young Māori offenders.

The concept of a Māori justice system, which is seen as a separatist threat to the status quo of Pākehā dominance and Māori subjection, needs clarification. The traditional system of Māori justice was based on the principle of utu, with its various meanings of payment, equivalence, compensation and revenge. Utu was attained by both spiritual and temporal means. Utu for an offence such as adultery was exacted by a taua muru, a raiding party which plundered the goods of an offender as compensation. Should such a measure be impolitic because of the danger of it escalating into fighting, then the aggrieved party could resort to mākutu to exact retribution by spiritual means. Mākutu was one way of exacting the death penalty for grievous offences without risk to the aggrieved party. Within a tribal community, behaviour was regulated by the all-pervading restrictions of tapu. Breaches against the laws of tapu exposed the mauri, the life force of an individual, to attack by demons. The offender sickened and in serious cases died. Intertribal relations were regulated by warfare. Trespass on garden land, fisheries and forest resources were all considered just causes for making war.

Colonisation, Christianity and cultural invasion have eroded this traditional system by dealing with offences to the point that they no longer exist. The leadership system of ariki, chiefs, tohunga and kaumātua, which maintained social control in the community by both spiritual and temporal means, has been tossed aside by Pākehā systems of management and control. There is today no Māori justice system extant in its own right, and Pākehā reap the consequences in Māori offending.

Despite the demise of the traditional system of justice, the demand for Māori autonomy in dealing with Māori offenders merits some consideration. In the immediate postwar years, the Māori Social and Economic Advancement Act 1945 gave tribal committees the power to constitute themselves as tribunals to deal with petty offences that disrupted community life. These tribunals operated within the social context of the tribe. They brought together the whānau of the offender and the offended party to discuss the conflict engendered by the offence and all its ramifications. Although the tribunals had power to impose fines up to $20, which they often did, punishment was secondary to the primary aim of resolving the conflict by arriving at a consensus. The aim was to restore social relations to the state of peace and harmony that prevailed before they were disrupted by the offence. This form of conflict resolution brought to bear the moral force of the tribal community on the offender. That moral force, and the conscience of the offender, are the main routes to reformation of offenders. All the evidence indicates that the punitive route is a judicial cul-de-sac.

After 1962, when the bulk of the Māori population moved to towns and cities, the Māori Welfare Act replaced the former act under which Māori tribunals operated. The tribal committees were displaced by 'Māori committees' to take cognisance of the multitribal situation. Some committees continued to operate tribunals in the urban context, but they were discouraged by officers of the Department of Māori Affairs, who disparaged them as 'kangaroo courts'. Underlying this campaign to do away with Māori tribunals was a naive commitment to the ideology of 'one people', which now has been exposed as a false consciousness. By 1970, Māori tribunals had virtually died out.

Māori tribunals were not separatist. They were part of the legal system, which gave ordinary people a role to play in the administration of justice at the community level. The tribunals co-operated with the authorities, and were obliged by the law to give defendants the option of accepting their jurisdiction or going to a higher court. What they offered was a Māori way of dealing with conflict resolution. In view of the Government's policy of devolution of resources and management of tribal affairs to iwi authorities, perhaps the time is opportune for it to reconsider the reinstatement of the judicial powers the tribes once had.

1 August 1989
(*Listener*)

Sexploitation

D OMINANT MALES taking sexual advantage of powerless or submissive females is a recurrent theme in Māori mythology and traditions. In the creation myth, the god Tāne created Hineahuone, the earth-formed maid, and cohabited with her to beget a daughter named Hinetītama, the Dawn Maid. He then cohabited with Hinetītama to beget other children. In due course, Hinetītama asked Tāne who her father was. He evaded the question by telling her to ask the pillars of their house. Hinetītama knew intuitively that her own husband was her father. She fled from him to the underworld to become Hinenuitepō, the goddess of death. Her flight and trans-formation dramatised the serious nature of Tāne's offence. It established the convention concerning the incest taboo, and the damage it does to family relations.

During the era of the great Polynesian navigators who roamed the Pacific before migrating to New Zealand, some of the most able navigators went from island to island for no more noble purpose than to couple with different women. One of these was Ironuimaota, a high-born chief with bloodlines connecting him to the Marquesas, Tahiti, and Samoa. He was the great lover who stole the wives of other men and left the cuckolds lamenting:

E Iro e, e Iro e, taoki mai taku va'ine e, ka mate au i te akama.
Oh, Iro, Oh, Iro, return my wife to me, for I die of shame.

In the end, his sexual peccadilloes brought him down and he fled to the distant colony of Aotearoa, where he is known as Whironui, the ancestor of the Ngāti Porou tribe of the East Coast.

Sexploitation of women continued in Aotearoa. Different tribes have their own stories. Among the Tainui, a peripatetic chief named Kōkako arrived at a spring and settled down to rest. During the night, the local princess in a nearby village got thirsty. She went to the spring where she was accosted by Kōkako, who forced his attentions on her. On his departure he instructed her, 'If your child is born a boy, then name him Tamainupō' (son conceived of a thirst in the night).

A similar story is told among the Arawa of their ancestor Uenukukopako loving and leaving a local woman at Te Teko with the instruction to name the child Rangiteaorere (cloud drifting by) if it was a boy.

A culture with sexploitation built into its myths and traditions indicates it was a deeply rooted practice. Such a practice was unlikely to be affected by modernity or conversion to Christianity. It continued unabated into our own times. In the end, the women cried enough. The first to bring the hidden sin out into the open was Dame Mira Szaszy when she was President of the Māori Women's Welfare League. She established a refuge for victims of incest and sexual abuse.

Almost a decade passed before men were confronted head on by Titewhai Harawira at a national hui at Tūrangawaewae Marae. She pushed through a resolution calling on all men to stop sexually abusing young women.

Men were slow to catch on. The practice continued, even at a time when the outrage of women in general was bringing pressure to bear on politicians and employers to stop sexual harassment.

Eventually, a group of innovative, action-oriented women in the Waikato put up the weights of seven kaumātua by denouncing them on the marae. They were stripped of their speaking rights on the paepae. The shame, the ignominy of being talked about, the denial of a pre-rogative so vital to male mana in a community of intense face-to-face relations with kith and kin is tantamount to living death. On every public occasion when visitors come to the marae, the shame is renewed. Only death can bring release from unrelieved public shame. What better punishment is there? Twenty years in jail at public expense? Out of sight, out of mind. Soon forgotten as the news of conviction becomes tomorrow's fish-and-chips wrapping.

What a fuss the story created in the newspapers when it

broke. Uninformed, ethnocentric claptrap about 'separate' justice. For the victims, there was no justice until the community took matters into its own hands. The victims of the secret sins of society are hardly likely to complain to the police about a father, brother, uncle or cousin over sexual molestation. The women who formed the victim's support group Kokonga Ngākau (corner of the heart) knew that, so they did their own thing.

Private settlement of disturbances in the community should be seen as an adjunct rather than as a threat to the judicial system. In any case, there are precedents, backed by statute for community-based tribunals as adjuncts to the judicial system. They are not separatist.

Surprisingly, of all the pundits asked to comment, the closest to intuit what is described above was the Prime Minister, Mr Bolger. He said peer pressure is a very significant deterrent to misbehaving in all its forms, especially where marae exercised considerable moral authority.

24 September 1993
(*Metro*)

The kiore

MORE THAN a year ago, University of Auckland scientists warned officers of the Department of Conservation (DOC) of the need to consult tāngata whenua over its plan to eradicate the kiore (*Rattus exulans*) on a number of offshore islands. Recently that warning was sheeted home to DOC by Te Warena Taua, spokesman for the Kawerau tribe. Taua was surprised to learn at a meeting of the Auckland Conservation Board that his tribe had given approval for the eradication of the kiore on Tiritiri Mātangi island in the Hauraki Gulf. DOC's rationale for the Tiritiri eradication programme is to create a sanctuary for endangered species. Although there is circumstantial evidence that the kiore has had some impact on indigenous flora and fauna, it is not an open-and-shut case. The endangered saddleback, for instance, which was introduced to Tiritiri from the mainland, has thrived on the island along with the kiore.

At issue are the contrasting values Māori and Pākehā have toward the kiore and its larger and more voracious cousins the ship rat (*Rattus rattus*) and the Norwegian rat (*Rattus norvecicus*). European culture has a long history of rat-borne diseases such as typhus and bubonic plague. Between A.D. 1346 and 1352, Europe lost almost a third of its population, approximately twenty million people, to the plague. The identification of rats as the bearers of pestilence engendered the concept of extermination as the only rational way for humans to relate to rats. The arch-exterminator embodied in European mythology was the Pied Piper of Hamlin. In New Zealand, we have DOC as the exterminator. DOC has a mandate from the Pākehā – but not the tāngata whenua – to exterminate rats.

In contrast to the European, the Māori and their Polynesian forebears had a positive relationship with the kiore, which is attested to by their migrations across the Great Ocean of Kiwa being accompanied by the kiore. The kiore, which originated from mainland southeast Asia, was carried as cargo on Polynesian vessels along with the pig, chicken and dog. Had the kiore been a stowaway like the ship rat, its distribution should have become attenuated along the east-west, north-south axes of the Polynesian migratory routes from Samoa to the Marquesas, north to Hawaii and south-west to New Zealand.

The widespread distribution of the kiore in the Pacific suggests that it was a valued possession, which the navigators took with them from island to island. This is confirmed by a study of Māori traditions concerning the kiore by Bradford Māka Hāmi. According to the Taranaki tribes, the kiore was brought from Hawaiki to New Zealand by Tūri on his ocean-going vessel the *Aotea*.

Tribes in the Far North also claim their ancestor Ruanui brought the kiore with him on the vessel *Mamāri*. Ruanui released his kiore on an island, subsequently known as Motukiore, in the Hokianga Harbour. When Ruanui returned to Hokianga from his exploration of the country, he found the kiore had disappeared from the island. He recited a karakia to bring them back, whereupon the kiore came out of the forest and swam back to Ruanui. This ancestor is depicted with pet kiore on his shoulder in Tānenuiarangi, the meeting house on the University of Auckland marae, and in Te Ōhaki house at Ahipara.

Given the Taranaki and Northland traditions concerning the origin of the kiore, it is not surprising that some of the sub-tribes in these areas regarded the kiore as an important food resource. Each sub-tribe had its own rāhui kiore, reserves where the kiore was trapped for food. The kiore was particularly fat and succulent when it fed on bush berries such as the taraire, tawa and miro. The miro berry imparted a highly seasoned flavour to the flesh of the kiore.

Among the Tūhoe people of the Urewera, the kiore was a prized delicacy cooked as potted preserves in its own fat and served as food for chiefs. Because of the custom of honouring visitors with huahua (preserved) kiore, Tūhoe were given the sobriquet 'Tūhoe kai kiore' by outsiders. According to Tūhoe tradition, they hunted the kiore, along with the mutton bird, around the cliffs on the shores of Waikaremoana. But with the arrival of the ship rat in historic times, both the kiore and the mutton bird disappeared from their territory. These events are recorded in Tūhoe waiata.

The kiore disappeared from the mainland altogether in the nineteenth century because it could not compete with the ship rat and the Norwegian rat. With the exception of Ngāi Tahu, who mount annual mutton-birding expeditions to offshore islands in the south, few Māori in the North Island knew the kiore was still extant. Had the tribes known that DOC had exterminated kiore on nine of the forty-eight islands on which they survived, then perhaps they would have been able to intervene, and make suggestions to ameliorate the programme on cultural grounds

Because Māori have not been properly informed, the challenge to DOC's eradication programme has been led by Dr Mere Roberts, a zoologist who studied the kiore for her dissertation. Roberts and her colleagues Professors Euan Young and John Craig argue that DOC's emphasis on

eradication should be balanced by a management programme for the kiore, in which the values of tāngata whenua
are taken into account through consultations with iwi for
whom the kiore has cultural significance. They argue that
some of the offshore islands should be set aside as kiore
reserves for scientific as well as cultural reasons. Furthermore, there is considerable research focussed on mito-
chondrial DNA tracing of ancestral origins of the Māori by
studying the plants and animals they transported from
island to island. In the long-term, these studies, in which
the kiore is one of the components, should enable scientists
to get a more accurate fix on the origins of the Māori.

24 April 1993
(*Metro*)

Lone pine

MEN DIE, mountains endure. Trees die, too. The tree
on Maungakiekie will die, just as the tree that
preceded it died. But before it dies we must ponder
what to do, because what we do to requite it, and what went
before, will be a statement of what we might become as a
nation.

Maungakiekie is one of the largest earth fortifications in
the South Pacific. In prehistoric times, it was the seat of
power of the Waiohua chief Kiwi Tāmaki. His mother,
Tahuri, cultivated extensive kūmara gardens at the base of
the fortress. They were named Ngā Mahinga a Tahuri. Kiwi
Tāmaki was a powerful chief, who thought his hold on
Tāmaki Makaurau was invincible. It was the most desirable
piece of real estate in Aotearoa, being at the nodal point of
water-borne traffic from Pēwhairangi in the north to Waikato
in the south. Marauding Ngāpuhi expeditions bent on
plundering southern tribes assembled their fleets at
Pēwhairangi, picked up reinforcements at Whangārei, and
sailed south into the Waitemata. At the head of the Tāmaki
estuary, the vessels were portaged across to the Manukau.
From there they made their way out to sea and entered the

Waikato Heads to have the heart of the island at their disposal.

Tāmaki was coveted for its rich volcanic soil, the two harbours with abundant fishlife, and the bushclad Waitakere Range to the north-west and Hūnua Range to the south. The inhabitants of the isthmus were also favoured by the presence of numerous volcanic cones, which were readily transformed into defensive systems, the most notable being Ōwairaka, Maungawhau, Maungarei, and, of course, Maungakiekie.

When Ngāti Whātua from the North conquered the Kaipara tribes, they had no desire to encroach south of the Waitakere Range. Nor did they want to antagonise the powerful Kiwi Tāmaki. They tried to placate him by inviting him to the tangi of one of their chiefs. Kiwi accepted the invitation, all the time plotting treachery. At the funerary feast, his men drew concealed weapons and decimated their hosts. As the Ngāti Whātua chief Wahākiaki fled, Kiwi cursed him saying he would hang his breastbone on Tōtara i ahua, the sacred tree where the trophies of war were hung at Maungakiekie.

Wahākiaki avenged the insult when he killed Kiwi Tāmaki at the Battle of Paruroa on the north-west edge of the Manukau Harbour. His ally Tuperiri pressed the attack home as one by one the fortresses of Tāmaki fell. The campaign ended with the occupation of Maungakiekie by Tūperiri.

Ngāti Whātua were the masters of Tāmaki. They were at the height of their power. But, as with Kiwi Tāmaki, nothing in the affairs of men is forever. Two generations later, the world of Ngāti Whātua was changed irrevocably by the arrival of Captain James Cook. More ships followed, and the isthmus was devastated by a series of epidemics. The strongholds of Maungawhau and Maungakiekie were abandoned.

In the 1820s, Ngāti Whātua's hold on Tāmaki was weakened further by the musket wars visited on them by Hongi Hika. Although Hongi did not occupy Tāmaki, Tūperiri's grandson Apihai Te Kawau lived in exile among his northern kin. He periodically visited Ōrākei to plant gardens and keep his ahi kā burning on the land. It was this 'warm' title to the land that enabled him to sell 3,000 acres, on which the city of Auckland stands, to Captain Hobson in November 1840. Safe from Ngāpuhi guns under the umbrella of *pax Britannica*, Apihai Te Kawau returned to Ōrākei.

In December 1840, John Logan Campbell, the so-called 'father of Auckland', arrived and set up in business at the foot of what is now Queen St, with his partner William Brown. As he prospered, his gaze soon fell on Maungakiekie. He noticed that this magnificent monument of a bygone age was adorned with a lone tree, the sacred Tōtara i ahua. The tree had been planted on the summit around 1600 to mark the burial place of the whenua, the afterbirth and umbilical cord, of the chief Koroki. Hence the name Tōtara i ahua, the symbolic image of Koroki. To name is to claim, and so, without any reference to the niceties of the past, Campbell named it One Tree Hill. It soon came into his possession when he bought the surrounding thousand acres in 1853.

By the time Campbell acquired One Tree Hill, it was already bereft of the tōtara, which had been wantonly cut down by Pākehā workmen. The act was a metaphor for colonisation as the native tōtara was replaced by exotic pines.

In 1901, Campbell donated 230 acres of his One Tree Hill estate to the nation to mark the visit of the Duke and Duchess of Cornwall. Maungakiekie, along with the gardens of Tahuri, became Cornwall Park. When he died in 1912, Campbell was buried at the summit of One Tree Hill. His monument, surmounted by an obelisk, is also a metaphor for imperialism. It is a monumental form whose protype can be traced to the Egyptian temple of Karnach. Two of the four original obelisks were looted by imperialists. One stands at the Hippodrome in Istanbul and the other at the Place de la Concorde in Paris. The obelisk on One Tree Hill has a remarkable resemblance to those granite originals. It stands as a symbol of European domination alongside the lone pine that replaced the native tōtara.

Monuments such as Maungakiekie, the obelisk, and One

Tree Hill are static symbols of the past. Their aura of permanence belies the swirl of human history around them. Last month, the subjugated knowledge of the past came back to haunt us when Mike Smith hacked at the lone pine on One Tree Hill. History had gone full circle. But instead of recognising that the grand narrative of our colonial history can no longer be sustained, the city fathers have spent a fortune trying to salvage the tree. That too is a metaphor for trying to sustain the unstainable in human relations. Domination is no longer tenable in this post-modern age of multiple discourses. If Maungakiekie/One Tree Hill is to have symbolic meaning in our own time, replacing the tree before it dies must be a joint enterprise between the tāngata whenua and city fathers.

25 November 1994
(*Metro*)

8: MĀORI AND THE MEDIA

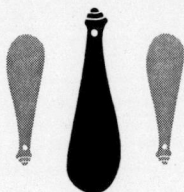

The role of the news media in defining Pākehā perceptions of the Māori

THE STRUCTURAL relationship that exists between the Māori as the tangāta whenua of New Zealand and Pākehā who settled the country in the last 150 years is one of social, political and economic subjection to the tyranny of majority rule. That relationship is derived from the historic process of colonisation of a tribal people, who had been isolated in the South Pacific for a thousand years, by the industrialised metropolitan nation of the United Kingdom.

Although the Māori stoutly resisted colonial despoliation by defending their land against invasion, by guerrilla warfare, petitions to the Queen for a Royal Commission to look into their grievances, and the formation of Māori parliaments, these efforts are not part of the psyche and collective memory of the Pākehā New Zealander. Because these events occurred mainly in the last century, they are confined to the dustbin of 'non-history'. As a consequence, the attempt at accommodation with the colonising power by educated Māori leaders such as Buck, Ngāta, and Pomare after the turn of the century was misunderstood by the Pākehā as acceptance by the Māori of their subordinate place in the new nation state. Māori participation in two world wars, integration in the national sport of rugby, combined with the isolation of Māori from Pākehā in rural tribal hinterlands, enabled the Pākehā to foster and promulgate to the world the myth of racial harmony in New Zealand.

That myth was shattered in the 1970s. By that time, 70 percent of the Māori population was urban. In the span of one generation, the centre of gravity of Māori society had shifted to towns and cities. In the urban milieu, there was an efflorescence of Māori culture in the development of culture clubs, Māori sports teams, and the building of urban marae. With the transition from rural to urban life accomplished, Māori people turned to political action in response to the dominating and suffocating presence of Pākehā power-brokers in their lives.

Urbanisation gave the Māori increased knowledge of the nature and alienating power structures of urban society. Politicisation by urban-educated radicals saw widespread Māori engagement in transforming action. Public perception of the rising tide of Māori activism as one of young radicals disturbing harmony, and dividing the races, was fostered by the news media treatment of activism. In this respect, the Fourth Estate, as an integral component of the Establishment, functioned to maintain the status quo and the structural relationship of Māori subordination. In other words, in dealing with issues across racial boundaries, the muchvaunted objectivity of newspapers stands on shaky foundations.

Contemporary Māori activism began with the emergence in 1970 of Ngā Tamatoa, the Young Warriors. Their annual protest at the Treaty of Waitangi celebrations triggered the Māori Land March in 1975, and the occupation of Bastion Point in 1977. Both the land march and Bastion Point protests were marked by passive resistance and accordingly treated in a benign manner by the state and the news media. But in 1979, a small group of activists, who for years had attempted by negotiation to stop the racist parody of the haka by the engineering students of the University of Auckland, resorted to violent action. Passive resistance is one thing but violence is another. The coloniser knows all too well the potential of violence for social transformation, for it was through violence that a tribal society was destroyed and the nation state of New Zealand brought into being. It is for that reason that the state has the monopoly on violence, because it is the means by which control and national security are maintained. Control means each class, race, and person functioning according to their assigned social role in the polity of the nation. The 'haka party' incident was perceived as a threat to control and the structurally assigned place of Māori subordination to Pākehā power. All this was implicit in the media treatment of the incident.

In May 1979, the *Auckland Star* reported the haka-party incident with the bold headlines 'Gang rampage at varsity' and 'Students at haka practice bashed'. The headline was sensationalist and inaccurate. Although there was not one gang patch in evidence on any one of those involved in the raid on the university, no headline could have evoked a more emotive response from the general public. The patch-wearing gang member is the nightmare incarnation of the worst fears of the Pākehā.

The first gang to appear on the Auckland scene in 1970 was the Stormtroopers, whose denim uniforms and swastika emblems symbolised their alienation from mainstream society. Thereafter, other gangs such as Black Power, Mongrel Mob, and Headhunters came to notice as they engaged in fraternal gang raids and battles over territory. As long as their aggression was internal, no one was too fussed. But a gang invading the hallowed precincts of the university was intolerable.

Public outrage fostered by media treatment demanded retribution. Editors pontificated – 'No place for violence' (*NZ Herald*, 3 May 1979), 'A racial farce' (*Dominion*, 4 May). Prominent Māori leaders such as Mr Dansey, the race relations conciliator, and Dr Sharples, his executive officer, came under immediate pressure from newspapers to disavow violence and thereby isolate the offenders as social outcasts. The headline for their comments on the issue read 'Attack on students condemned' (*NZ Herald*, 2 May). One had to read the small print to discover Sharples's rider to his disapproval of violence that most of Māoridom would support the stand against the haka. It was not until the *Auckland Star* (28 May) reported the Auckland District Māori Council's reasons for providing 'Māori help for the haka attack group' that it was made clear that there was anything other than a Pākehā view on the incident. Even so, when the haka-party case went to court, it was reported as a 'lighthearted' stunt (*NZ Herald*, 6 July; *Auckland Star*, 6 July). Only two writers put the issue in its correct context of racism. These were W. P. Reeves' radical view 'Rough ride to racism' (*Dominion*, 18 May), and Tony Reid's editorial 'Mocking the Māori' (*NZ Listener*, 26 May). It was not until after the court hearing against the He Taua defendants, when respectable Māori leaders mounted a presence at court and argued the case of cultural violence by Pākehā students precipitating physical violence in retaliation, that the press understood the issue. When the Human Rights Commission produced its report on the incident, more discerning headlines began to appear, such as 'Cherished myth of racial harmony', 'After the haka . . . whither New Zealand?' (*NZ Herald*, 10 April 1980), 'The haka party incident and beyond' (*Auckland Star*, 10 April).

Although Pākehā perceptions of the haka-party affair as a one-off incident changed in the end, the general structural relationship of Pākehā dominance and complacency toward the Māori remained intact. A year later, when young activists resorted to dramatising Māori land grievances in the play *Marangā Mai*, performed at Māngere College in Auckland, the negative response of some Pākehā to it was, like the haka party, given prominent treatment. The *Herald* headline of 3 May 1980 read 'School angry after show by Māori group'. Equally sensational was the headline 'Angry minister calls for ban on play group' (*Auckland Star*, 5 May). The play, which for dramatic effect used 'bad language', reputedly disturbed 'race feelings' and led to Mr Wellington, the Minister of Education, calling on the Manukau City Council to ban the *Marangā Mai* theatrical performance from schools in its area.

The opinion of a Pākehā city councillor, Mr Peter

Aldridge, on Māori reaction was given prominent treatment in the headline 'Māori parents intimidated on play' (*Auckland Star*, 7 May). Mr Aldridge's right to speak on behalf of Māori was not challenged by the press. Nor was the slant of the headline negated by the small-print treatment given to the opinion of the President of the Labour Party, Jim Anderton, that the violent reaction to the play should be 'treated with the contempt it deserved' (*Auckland Star*, 7 May).

The power of the press to put a negative slant on Māori actions aimed at redressing their grievances precipitated a witchhunt. The *Herald* ran the headline 'Manukau Council wants report on show' (6 May). The actions of the city council's detached youth worker Brian Lepou in arranging the play's performance was closely scrutinised by the City Manager. The Department of Internal Affairs, which paid Lepou's salary, was asked to investigate the matter as well. This overreaction by Pākehā authorities to the *Maranga Mai* performance, and slanted sensationalist treatment of it in the press, can only be interpreted as Pākehā intolerance of Māori attempts to confront them with the past. They well knew the power of drama, however amateurishly presented, to change people's political perceptions. Faced with a challenge to the status quo of Pākehā dominance and Māori subordination, the power-brokers and the media made common cause in their loud public condemnation of *Maranga Mai*.

By the time the play reached its finale at a special performance in the Beehive theatrette four months later, the negative public perception of it was solidified by the headline 'Urban guerrilla play stuns Beehive' (*NZ Herald*, 2 September). That stated unequivocally the fear underlying Pākehā opposition to *Maranga Mai*, that Māori activism and politicisation would generate revolt against Pākehā hegemony.

For ten years Māori protest activity at the annual Treaty of Waitangi celebrations provided the press with good copy and ample ammunition to portray the protesters in a negative light. In 1981, when the investiture of Dame Whina

Cooper and Sir Graham Latimer was held on Waitangi Marae, the press had a field-day. The protesters objected to the investiture taking place on the marae, and the presence of the Governor-General, whose predecessors had dishonoured the Treaty. The noisy but peaceful protest was characterised as a 'full-scale riot', with the headline 'Waitangi Marae in uproar as police arrest eight' (*NZ Herald*, 7 February 1981). The *Star* similarly reported in bold headlines 'Police, activists brawl on marae' (*Auckland Star*, 6 February).

Police overreaction in arresting protesters for crying 'shame' during the investiture was justified by police going into what they declared 'an emergency situation because people's lives were at stake. It could have erupted in a full-scale riot.' Television coverage of the protest with shots of people milling about on the marae, combined with newspaper reportage of the incident, reinforced public perception of the protest as a violent affair. The depiction of the protesters as villains in the socio-drama between Māori and Pākehā on that Waitangi Day was given credence by the papers promulgating Prime Minister Muldoon's view that the protesters were 'outcasts' in Māori society (*NZ Herald*, 7 February).

Ten months after the event, the riot charges against the seven protesters arrested at Waitangi were dismissed in the Kaikohe District Court. Judge Paul's finding that not one stone had been thrown, nor any stick wielded in a manner that would constitute a riot, did nothing to disperse the original public perception of the protest at Waitangi being other than violent. For those who were present, and who read Mr Paul's judgement, it was evident the media had clearly distorted public perception of reality by the lax use of their power to mould and to define the context of social events. The net effect, whether conscious or otherwise, is that, in dealing with conflict between Māori and Pākehā, the Fourth Estate buttressed the position of the power elites and reinforced Pākehā dominance and Māori subjection. The transformation sought by the activists is accordingly delayed.

While the activists were the cutting edge of Māori society seeking social change, gangs as organisations for the dispossessed, alienated, brown proletariat, were the Achilles heel, vulnerable to Pākehā counter-attack. In the seventies, as gang fights raged over territory, the police operated as neutral observers, intervening only when necessary to investigate homicides from these wars, or robberies committed by gangs. But in 1979, when the Stormtroopers were unable to track down their rivals to do battle with them, the police became the object of their drunken rage when a nasty confrontation occurred in the carpark of the Moerewa hotel.

It culminated in violent assault on police, the burning of a police van, and the shooting of a gang member. Headlines such as 'Kill, kill, kill!', 'Northland nurses its wounds after a weekend of violence' (*NZ Herald*, 6 August), and 'Shotguns trained on gangs' (*Auckland Star*, 6 August), while calculated for their maximum sensational effect, also roused deep fears and hostility in the general populace towards gangs. Even the President of the Māori Council felt impelled to call for a 'crackdown' on gang violence (*NZ Herald*, 28 October 1980).

By the time the Government committee on gangs, chaired by Mr Comber, Under-Secretary for Internal Affairs, reported in May 1981, the heat surrounding the affairs had been somewhat dissipated by community meetings in Northland, revelations of high unemployment, and commentaries by researchers and detached youth workers assigned to gangs. The violence was seen as not gratuitous, but symptomatic of complex underlying social problems arising out of family breakdown, alienation, school failure and unemployment.The Comber Committee report warned that the news media was responsible for promulgating 'more negative images of gangs' than was justified. It said a cursory study of news media coverage suggested it focused on gangs as a high-profile issue at times which led to intense but poorly balanced coverage of gang-related issues (*NZ Herald*, 13 May).

Despite that observation by the Comber Committee, the enduring public perception of gangs is one of bestial behaviour and gratuitous violence. The Mongrel Mob reinforced that perception when a young woman was snatched off the street in Māngere at the gang's Ambury Park convention in 1986 and raped. In recent years reports of rape have become common. With the exception of the National Organisation of Women and women who staff the Auckland Rape Crisis Centre, the crime of rape barely raises comment. But the gang rape at Ambury Park became a *cause célèbre* in the newspapers. Gang violation of females was seen as so much more reprehensible than individual rape. Outraged citizens of Māngere, mainly Pākehā males, threatened dire consequences to members of the Auckland Regional Authority for permitting the use of Ambury Park for a gang convention. The community was reported to be 'Out for ARA blood' (*NZ Herald*, 15 December). Members of Parliament urged government action to give police stronger powers to deal with gangs (*NZ Herald*, 16 December).

The political ripples at the local level were much more compelling. Leaders felt obliged to take their own punitive action against the gang, irrespective of what the law did in bringing the guilty individuals to justice. The whole gang, comprised of chapters from all over the country, was to bear the stigma of the event. The Chairman of the Auckland Regional Authority Parks Committee threatened retaliation against the Auckland chapter of the Mongrel Mob with a loss to its Ngā Kurī Rohe Pōtae work trust of a three-months, $30,000 contract (*Auckland Star*, 16 December).

This chapter of the Mob, under the leadership of Tūhoe Isaacs, had called for a moratorium on criminal offending in an attempt to establish a work trust for his members to emulate the achievement of the successful Black Power gang with its work trust, 'factory' and night club headquarters in East Tāmaki. The report 'Gang finds pride through work', with the Black Power leader Abe Wharewaka quoted as saying 'Business turns me on' (*NZ Herald*, 15 November), was the one positive portrayal of gangs in thousands of words written about them over a ten-year period. But that was negated by the Ambury Park rape, and the hysteria generated over it in the media. It was a grave setback to the

Auckland chapter of the Mongrel Mob's plans to bring its members back into mainstream society because the 'credibility of the gang', according to Mr Curtis, Mayor of Manukau City, 'had been destroyed' (*NZ Herald*, 15 December).

Meanwhile, in the South Island the police declared its own open season on gangs with a 'Police probe on gang work schemes' (*NZ Herald*, 15 October 1986) even though the Labour Department, which administered the work schemes, had not lodged a complaint of impropriety. The work schemes were characterised in one press report quoting a policeman as 'a pipeline to Treasury for the gangs' (*NZ Herald*, 15 October). Contracts ranging from $90,000 up to $900,000 were quoted as having been siphoned off as benefits to the gangs. Although the Government's Project Employment Programme was designed for the unemployed, the money spent on the scheme was characterised in one report as '$4 million spent on gang jobs' (*Sunday Times*, 25 January 1987). The accretion of Mafia-like status to gangs by slanted news reports against gangs, and the publicity given to them by the leaked report of Sergeant Penn on his investigation into the work schemes, was hardly negated by the police censure of the Commander of the Invercargill Police district for leaking the incomplete report to the press (*NZ Herald*, 13 March).

Clearly, despite occasional reports and articles to the contrary, the primary image of gangs fostered by the media is a negative one. For this reason, gang-bashing can be indulged in by politicians, police, local bodies and newspapers without fear of being contradicted. Although there are only an estimated 2000 gang members throughout New Zealand, the continuous negative coverage of their activities by the press is felt as a discomfiture and embarrassment by 400,000 otherwise law-abiding Māori. The long-running denigration and criticism of gangs in the media functions for Pākehā as a constant reproach to Māori society, and a reminder of subordinate status, while at the same time providing sensational copy. In other words, gang-bashing in the media is a socially acceptable, oblique form of Māori-bashing. Pākehā gangs such as Highway 61 and Hell's Angels do not come in for the same attention.

While Māori gangs were given extensive media coverage for their anti-social behaviour, conservative Māori leaders were just as likely to come in for a bashing in newspapers for pursuing laudable social goals. The so-called 'Māori loans affair' is a case in point. In 1984, the Hui Taumata (summit conference) of Māori leaders recommended the establishment of a Māori Development Bank to enable Māori people to make a quantum leap forward economically to close the gap between Māori and Pākehā.

In pursuit of that resolution, the Secretary of Māori Affairs, Dr Tāmati Reedy, entered into negotiations with Hawaiian middle-men for an off-shore loan of $600 million at the discount interest rate of 6 percent. Despite the fact that the power to borrow such a sum resided only with the Minister of Finance, who stopped the loan negotiations under advice from Treasury on 24 November, the 'Māori loans affair' became another *cause célèbre* in the media for over two months.

The issue was raised in Parliament by Winston Peters, Opposition spokesman on Māori Affairs, in an attempt to discredit the Minister, Koro Wētere. The media rose to the bait like hungry sharks to foster speculation on the likely source of the loan, whether it was Arab money or 'Marcos millions' (*Auckland Star*, 17 December 1986; *NZ Herald*, 18 December). A parallel was drawn by the *Herald* with an 'earlier scandal' that 'blotted the career' of Sir Apirana Ngata (*NZ Herald*, 18 December). Like the village gossip rejoicing in scandal, one paper ran stories about 'New Zealand loan emissaries being two former bankrupts' (*Sunday Star*, 21 December) and a 'Key Māori loans man who ran broke companies' (*Star*, 18 December). An editorial warned that Māoridom had a 'taniwha by the tail' (*NZ Herald*, 18 December). Yet no such pontification was evident two years later as Pākehā investment companies lost billions of real dollars of investors' money in the wake of the sharemarket crash.

Māori people were shell-shocked by the unprecedented

level of Māori-bashing indulged in by the media over the so-called 'Māori loans affair' as headline followed headline. 'Māori Affairs in for shakeup come what may' wrote the *Herald* (19 December). 'Report on loan is whitewash say Nat MPs' (*Star*, 18 December). 'Maori leaders knew of the loans affair', claimed the *Herald* (19 December). 'PM calls on Mr Wetere to explain', wrote the *Herald* (6 July). 'Māori loan row not finished with yet', claimed the *Herald* (10 February 1987). 'Inquiry the only way out' argued the *Auckland Star* (10 February).

Although the Deane Report to Parliament two months previously had made it clear that the minister had stopped the loan, the press persisted. It had the Māori on the rack and was not about to release its victim. The loans affair had been so reified by the press that it had taken on a life of its own. Even when the Speaker of the House ruled in a breach of privilege case that the Minister, Mr Wētere, had not misled the House on the loans affair, and 'closed the lid' on the Peters-Wētere case (*Auckland Star*, 11 February), the media was reluctant to release its hapless victim. Seven months later the *Herald* (9 December) ran the story 'Second Māori loan affair looming'. Three months later, the *Star* attempted to resurrect the moribund theme with the story that the Audit Office hoped to complete its inquiry before Christmas into what has become known as 'the second Māori loans affair' (*Auckland Star*, 11 December). The preoccupation of the press for such a prolonged period with a loan that never occurred is explicable on two grounds. First, the manufacture of sensational news for public consumption and the maintenance of market share. Second is preservation of the structural relationship of Pākehā dominance and Māori subordination. Achievement of financial power by Māori posed a serious challenge to that relationship. The challenge was put down by overkill in the media.

Since 1985, when the Waitangi Tribunal's powers were made retrospective to 1840, Māori leaders have taken several steps aimed at redressing past injustices arising out of colonisation. There are presently 150 claims before the Tribunal, the two major ones being the Ngāi Tahu claim for the 'tenths' in the South Island, and the Tainui claim for the million acres confiscated for military settlers. These claims have roused deep-rooted fears of Pākehā dispossession.

Those fears were exacerbated in 1987 when the High Court granted the Māori Council's injunction claiming that the transfer of Crown lands to state-owned enterprises prejudiced claims before the Waitangi Tribunal. Five judges were unanimous that the Treaty of Waitangi overrode the State Owned Enterprises Act. Then, in October 1987, another injunction granted by Judge Greig recognised the Māori property right to fisheries under the Treaty of Waitangi by suspending the Government's Individual Transferable Quota fisheries management regime.

The Māori challenge for the return of their resources was now conducted on two fronts, land and sea. These challenges to reverse the Pākehā monopoly of resources on the basis of Treaty rights have resulted in heightened racial tension. The issue of race became another *cause célèbre* in the media, with most of the heat emanating from Pākehā, some of it bordering on paranoia.

Māori people have felt the pain of dispossession under the Treaty of Waitangi for 150 years. But before even one acre of land, or one cent of compensation, was returned to the Māori by the Waitangi Tribunal, the views of Pākehā crying foul were given prominence in newspapers. 'That Treaty? — scrap it and substitute another pact,' said Ralph Maxwell, Undersecretary for Agriculture and Fisheries (*NZ Herald*, 25 January 1988). Mr Bolger, Leader of the Opposition, argued that claims before the Waitangi Tribunal were starting 'to gnaw away' at [Pākehā] New Zealanders' (*NZ Herald*, 4 December 1987). He went on to claim he suspected 'bias' in the tribunal (*NZ Herald*, 13 February 1988). One editor joined the debate by asserting 'The Tribunal plays with dynamite' (*Auckland Star*, 27 January 1988).

Fear of Māori winning back some of their stolen resources in the courts, or through the Waitangi Tribunal, was readily translated by politicians such as Sir Robert Muldoon into 'Race relations fear' (*Sunday Star*, 20 March

1988). Although 'racist solutions' were 'rejected by party leader' Mr Bolger (*NZ Herald*, 6 August 1988), 'race issues' returned to 'haunt parties' (*NZ Herald*, 13 August 1988) on the occasion of the National Party Conference. The views of the member for Tauranga, Winston Peters, that the Treaty of Waitangi was outmoded and needed review, and that the party would target the Tribunal as an 'instrument of possible injustice to Pākehās', ventilated Pākehā feelings. These views, expressed on behalf of his Pākehā constituents, alienated Mr Peters from his Māori colleagues in the party.

Pākehā preoccupation with race as an issue in 1988 was fuelled by the gratuitous mistatement of the year from Hana Te Hemara, reported in bold headlines, 'Kill A White' (*Sunday Star*, 20 March). The media and the public fastened on it as evidence of their worst fears. Despite protestations by Te Hemara, that this was not what she advocated or meant to say, the damage was done. The Race Relations Office was deluged with complaints. When Mr Hirsh, the Race Relations Conciliator, ruled that the remark was outside section 9A of the Race Relations Act because it was made at a private function, there were demands for the abolition of the Race Relations Office. The *Sunday Star* fomented the issue by running the story for its sensational effect and in self-justification of the Pākehā view that Māori can be just as racist as themselves. The editor of the *Star* refused to apologise for publicising the statement which incited disharmony when called upon to do so by the Race Relations Conciliator.

The role of the media in publicising race as an issue *per se* in 1988, as if it were separate from the Māori challenge for equity and social justice, has had the effect of creating the social climate whereby politicians would be enabled to remove the source of Pākehā irritation with Māori people. In other words, the Treaty of Waitangi, and abolition of the Waitangi Tribunal are likely to be key political issues between Labour and National in the General Election of 1990.

28 February 1989
(Paper delivered at Race Relations Symposium on Māori in the Media)

The world according to Duff

AST SUMMER I read Alan Duff's second book *One Night Out Stealing*. I enjoyed it. Duff tells a good yarn, with powerful prose and compelling imagery. He is the only author I know who replicates in writing the patois of the lower strata. That is because he writes as a former insider with an intimate knowledge of the seamy side of life, with its boozing, brawling, and petty crime.

Duff's latest book, *Maori*, is neither fiction nor non-fiction. It purports to deal with 'the crisis and the challenge' facing the Māori today. But it is short on facts, and makes no reference to the extensive literature on the subject of the Māori. Because the book sits in isolation, as nothing more than the opinionated views of the author, it is also bereft of political analysis and social relevance. If the book has any relevance at all, it can only be as a reflection of what 'redneck' New Zealanders think of Māori. In this respect, it is more symptomatic of Pākehā New Zealand than it is of the reality of the Māori. Because the author feeds on the knowledge, prejudices and stereotypes of the common man, the book is self-confirming in its view of the Māori as a hopeless misfit in the modern world.

The key to understanding this book is chapter five, where the author reverts to the lower-class patois of his deprived background to paint the portrait of the Māori as a born loser. He argues the veracity of the case he makes on the basis of personal experience. There is no other reality than the world according to Duff.

It is clear from the author's familiarity with the social landscape of the housing estate that he was traumatised by the experience of parental neglect, drunkenness and violence. That experience, combined with general deprivation, compared to Pākehā counterparts, engendered deep-seated feelings of anger, resentment and self-hate.

For the author, there are no pluses in being Māori. The centre of gravity of his life is in the Pākehā world. That is where he is and wants to be. He would like other Māori to join him. Success as a novelist provided the author with an escape route from the world he despises. He advances education as the escape route for others as if it were a personal discovery. He asserts that Māori do not value education, in the face of evidence of students staying on longer at school and rising Māori enrolment in universities, polytechs, and colleges of education.

Last month, 150 Māori students graduated at Auckland University. The same number graduated at Waikato. The Auckland students were spread across arts, medicine, science, law and commerce. On the Saturday of capping week, the undergraduates honoured the graduates and their whānau with a presentation ceremony on the university marae. The remark of the day was made by a man with a tattooed face to a gathering of over 400 people: 'Alan Duff, eat your heart out.' It was greeted with much mirth.

Where once the author worked out his anger by punching up opposition to assert dominance, he now engages in verbal fisticuffs against Māori whose experience was different from his own. Māori leaders are dismissed as 'pig-ignorant' kaumātua, who place no value on the written word. This assertion is made in ignorance of extensive manuscript collections by kaumātua in the national and regional libraries. Although there is ample evidence of Māori productivity in farming and business enterprise, all Māori are dismissed as failures because they have no work ethic and are hooked on welfarism. There is no mention of multi-million dollar Māori enterprises such as farming and forestry incorporations, 438 trusts, Moana Pacific Fisheries, Māori Development Corporation, Quality Inns, Ubix, Deka, Power Beat, and Māori International.

Although the author claims to value education, and the written word, he has not made up for his own impoverished educational background by reading. It shows in his writing, which relies on dogmatic repetition rather than adducing facts to make a point. In the end, the author's dogmatism, and lack of intellectual rigour, betray him. Māori who obviously do have a work ethic, as evidenced by their success in education, business, or a profession, are not held up as role models. Instead, they are dismissed as radical, culture vultures, or mule-stubborn for being pro-Māori.

When he runs out of targets for his verbal hay-makers, the author resorts to erecting straw men and knocking them down. 'Will a haka explain the financial position to a board of directors? Will an ancient waiata persuade a bank to invest in a business venture? Will a long-winded speech in Māori do anything to assist a massive futures trade on the New York stock exchange?'

Duff's ego is so monumental that ignorance of a subject does not deter him from venturing an opinion, as long as it gives him a chance to put Māori people down. He denounces quota for university faculties with limited entry as racism rather than an attempt to create a level playing field. Last year, the field for entry into Auckland Medical School was destabilised by Asians taking 25 percent of direct entry places from secondary school. This year, entry criteria were altered to ensure Pākehā were admitted according to their proportion in society.

Māori is basically a reflection of cultural politics in New Zealand. It restates long-held views by Pākehā about Māori, which in recent years became distinctly unfashionable because of their racial overtones. But because a Māori is saying it, the book is at the top of the best-seller list. To the Māori, Duff is irrelevant. He does not rate in the Māori world because he is not part of the people's struggle for emancipation and social advancement. The intelligentsia sees him as a cultural renegade not worthy of being dignified by public comment. But to the Pākehā he represents the great white hope of turning back the dynamic of Māori self-determination.

15 May 1993
(*Metro*)

War and peace

L AST MONTH I saw the movie version of *Once Were Warriors*. It was one of the most stunning movies I have seen for a long time. I thought that the book which inspired it was flawed by the bleakness of its message and lack of human redemption. When Communicado acquired the movie rights to *Warriors*, most Māori thought that they were going to be done in again by a Pākehā construction of Māori as a bunch of no-hopers, given to drunkenness, violence and sexual deviance. But that negative view of a once-proud race of warriors fallen on evil days was turned around by one person, the producer Robin Scholes.

As a victim herself of violence and sexual attack at the hands of the Parnell panther Mark Stephens, no one had more reason to exact utu than Robin Scholes. Instead she chose to reconstruct the raw material of the novel into a moving commentary on the human condition. Scholes began by assembling an impressive array of Māori talent to work on the project. The list included scriptwriter Riwia Brown, director Lee Tamahori, casting director Don Selwyn, and leading actors Rena Owen and Temuera Morrison.

Implicit in Duff's *Warriors* is the imputation that the violence so graphically portrayed was derived from the warrior tradition. It was in the blood, like a genetic flaw. He was wont to expose it, to bring it out into the open, thereby precipitating a painful catharsis that would move people to extirpate it and expunge it from tribal memory. This simplistic view stemmed from Duff's own personal experience of bad parenting, alienation, and lack of knowledge about his own culture.

Māori males were not born warriors. They were trained to it, just as soldiers are trained. They were also gardeners, artists, hunters, fishermen, and housebuilders. In other words, they were trained in the peaceful arts as well as the arts of war. There were widely accepted conventions for making peace. These included the linking of tribes by the exchange of high-ranking women in marriage and the exchange of treasured heirlooms. The latter was known as tatau pounamu, the greenstone door.

In the past, there were checks and balances against capricious and violent behaviour towards women. If men beat their wives, they were answerable to their brothers-in-law, who could plunder a husband's property as compensation. Brothers-in-law would also make war on errant husbands if they thought it warranted. Even verbal abuse of women was considered just cause for war. Women were also able to desert unkind husbands and take refuge with their own tribe.

In former times, child-beating was alien to Māori culture. Children were loved and indulged, especially by their nannies. The nannies in the extended family would not countenance a child being chastised by their parents. Child homicide was rare. When it occurred it was for political reasons similar to the murder of the Princes in the Tower. Benevolent child-rearing practices persisted into the first half of this century. A study by Ernest and Pearl Beaglehole, in 1946, disapproved of Māori child-rearing practices as being too indulgent. According to the Beagleholes, Māori children were born into a 'golden world of affection'. They were the centre of adult attention and affection. They were fed on demand, self-willed, and not disciplined in any way. That was of course before the urban migration and the erosion of tribal structures.

Duff's lack of knowledge of his own culture comes out in the unidimensional nature of his writing. The flaws in the novel carried over into the first draft he wrote for the movie script of *Warriors*. Robin Scholes was not satisfied. Nor was the director, Lee Tamahori. Scholes resolved the problem by persuading Toby Curtis to join the project as cultural adviser. This was a smart move as both Curtis and Duff belong to the Arawa confederation of tribes. Duff, who had publicly rubbished kaumātua as 'pig ignorant', found that Curtis, although only a junior kaumātua, was far from 'pig ignorant'. He was unable to 'stuff the kaumātua' as he had proclaimed on television when he clashed with Curtis over the first and second drafts of the script. The clash of wills culminated in a third draft. Although it was an improvement on the first two, Scholes, Curtis and Tamahori were still not satisfied with it. Rather than continue the debate with a recalcitrant author bent on salvaging his book, Riwia Brown was engaged to rework the script. She turned it around by making it into a woman's movie on the universal theme of male violence against wife and family.

The focus of the story shifted from the violence of Jake Heke, who solved all problems with his fists, to his wife Beth. In the end, Beth found the courage to leave her husband and save herself and her children from destruction. Although Beth was the heroine of the movie, throughout there was the menacing presence of Jake, superbly played by Temuera Morrison. I have not been enamoured of Morrison's acting as Dr Rōpata in *Shortland Street*. *Warriors* reveals why he is not convincing as Dr Rōpata. Dr Rōpata is a Māori part written by a Pākehā author for a Pākehā soap. The author fails to get inside the Māori skin with the result that Morrison is not comfortable in the part. Jake, on the other hand, is a Māori character written by a Māori for a Māori actor. Playing Jake brought out the latent acting talent in Morrison. His performance is even more creditable when his small stature is related to the physical presence he managed to project on screen.

The veteran actor George Hēnare also contributed to the movie in a cameo role as the welfare officer. His urbanity and BBC English was a counterfoil to the coarse language of Jake and his pub mates. He also provided a masterly touch in his weaponry display with the taiaha. The hau, the swish of the divine wind of the weapon, brought meaning to the warrior tradition implied in the title *Once Were Warriors* but absent in the book. In this respect the movie is a better reflection of reality than the book which inspired it.

28 June 1994
(*Metro*)

9: EDUCATION AND POWER

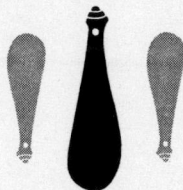

Education and power

KNOWLEDGE IS a form of power, which the ruling class control and monopolise. Theoretically, education is the avenue for upward mobility for intelligent members of lower strata. But, in reality, education operates a gate-keeping system of certification and credentialling, which keeps the structural relations of inequality in place. Intellectuals from subordinate strata are, by their education, infected with bourgeois values. They are readily recruited as subalterns to the ruling class. The subalterns exercise functions of social hegemony and political government.[1]

In the nineteenth century, European expansion into the new world set in train the historic process of colonisation and subjection of the tāngata whenua, the first nations, the people of the land. The common experience around the Pacific rim included population decline induced by epidemic diseases carried by the coloniser, conversion to Christianity, treaty-making, military invasion, cultural and language suppression, and political subjection. Because the first nations are ethnically distinct from the invaders, they are invariably relegated to the lowest strata of the new nation state. They score lowest on the social indices of health, life expectancy, education and employment.

The New Zealand experience

Tribal leaders in Aotearoa wanted access to the knowledge that made Europeans great, the knowledge that produced ships, powerful weapons and a cornucopia of material goods. That desire for access was thwarted in the mission schools where instruction in reading and writing was confined to the native language. That way, education was limited to scriptural material only, and access to secular knowledge denied.[2]

Clearly, knowledge is a form of power, and those who control the curriculum of education are able to determine its outcome. To the Christian mission of conversion was added the Governor's agenda of assimilation. In 1847, the state subsidised the mission schools to isolate Māori children from what the Governor condemned as the 'demoralising influences' of their villages.[3]

In 1867, the Government decided that the thirteen schools run by the Anglican, Catholic and Wesleyan missions had failed to break the 'communism' of the villages.[4] It mounted its own programme to assimilate Māori by establishing native schools in tribal areas. Because teaching was in English instead of the native language, progress was slow. After the turn of the century, the authorities banned the use of Māori in school precincts. For five decades, corporal punishment enforced the suppression of the native language. The schools became sites of resistance to cultural invasion and domestication.

In this dismal scenario of Māori education, the Anglican boarding school Te Aute College stood out as a model. It succeeded where others had failed because the aims of the principal, John Thornton, coincided with the aspirations of the people. He provided a matriculation programme to enable young Māori men to go on to university to study law, medicine and the arts. The outcome was the first wave of Māori graduates who entered politics between 1905 and 1911 to get a better deal for their people. Dr Pomare and Dr Buck instituted health reforms, which helped the population to recover. Sir Apirana Ngata promoted a cultural renaissance and instituted the first Māori land development scheme when he became Minister of Native Affairs in 1928.

As long as the Māori intelligentsia exercised subaltern functions, they were indulged and rewarded with knight-hoods. But when Ngata began empowering his own people by replacing Pākehā supervisors with Māori ones on his land schemes, the bureaucracy turned against him. His schemes were vilified in the press as a 'waste of Pākehā money'. After a Commission of Inquiry found two of Ngata's supervisors culpable of falsifying accounts, he resigned his portfolio in 1934.[5]

Long before Ngata moved to empower his own people, the intellectual elite of the ruling class foresaw the danger of Māori intellectuals competing with Pākehā for status and resources. The Director of Education decreed that the curriculum of native schools would be weighted in favour of handwork, manual skills and technical instruction. His department tried to persuade Te Aute College to replace its matriculation programme with agricultural training. The Inspector of Native Schools argued that the object of education was to fit pupils for life among Māori. They were not to mingle with Europeans and compete with them in trade and commerce.[6] He convinced Hukarere College, a boarding school for girls, to replace its academic subjects with needlework, cooking and domestic work. The object of education for girls was to train them to become 'good wives and mothers'.[7] The professor of biology at Victoria University College advocated manual training below the level of artisan and practical farming on strictly limited lines.[8]

The Education Department's policy of controlling the curriculum in Māori schools to deny access to tertiary education and the professions was continued into the 1950s. The curriculum of Māori district high schools included metalwork, cooking, home management, decorating and infant welfare for girls.[9] In 1945, Māori parents realised they were being short-changed by the education system. They requested that School Certificate courses be taught in their schools as well as in the general high schools.

The educational oppression of Māori by the ruling class

had a necrotic effect. Between 1900 and 1960, fluency in the native language fell from 95 percent to 25 percent.[10] Because school was an arena of oppression and cultural conflict, there was a gap of fifty years between the first and second wave of Māori graduates. This gap was identified in 1960 as a 'statistical blackout' by the Hunn Report.[11] Over 85 percent of students left secondary school with no educational qualification. For this reason, there were only eighty-nine undergraduates at university when there should have been eight times that number.

The high schools were the choke-point that allowed only a thin trickle of Māori into tertiary education. The primary impediment in the native schools was the inferior curriculum laid down by the Education Department. But with the urban migration in the post-war years, the arena of conflict shifted from the native to the general schools. Minority status, low teacher expectations, alienation, social breakdown of extended family support, and racial conflict made high schools uncongenial places for Māori pupils. The pupils responded by truanting. The schools reacted by suspending or expelling them. By the second year of high school, the drop-out rate was 30 percent. By the third year, it was 80 percent. Only exceptional students went on to higher education.

The radical potential of Māori to reform education

As victims of colonisation, cultural imperialism and proletarianisation through educational suppression, Māori had a radical potential to reform education. That potential first became manifest in the 1960s. The Māori intellectuals who insinuated themselves into the teaching profession tried to reform the education system from within. They believed it was possible to transform a monocultural education system, and its underlying ideology of assimilation, to incorporate the bicultural perspective of the Māori. The intellectuals thought that making schooling more congenial and user-friendly to Māori would encourage students to stay on at school. Underlying this strategy was an assumption of goodwill on the part of the ruling class towards Māori intellectuals who were their subalterns in the education system.

Co-operative strategies for bridging the education gap included fund-raising for the Māori Education Foundation, introducing Māori language and culture into the curriculum, establishment of homework centres, forming Māori education advancement committees, and enthusiastic adoption of the play-centre system of pre-school training. These strategies were essentially responses to the deficit theories that Māori were 'culturally deprived',[12] they spoke a 'restricted language' code and did not know their own language.

After twenty-five years of trying to reform the education system from within to make it bicultural, Māori leaders realised that the co-operative strategy was not effective. The education gap between Māori and Pākehā, as measured by School Certificate passes, had hardly closed.[13] Even with the introduction of single-subject passes, 75 percent of Māori students were still leaving school with no qualifications. The organic intellectuals realised there was something more fundamental at work in the nature of New Zealand society that produced this constantly negative result.[14] Eventually, the intellectuals drew the conclusion that the problem was structural rather than cultural. The root cause was unequal power relations between Māori and Pākehā in a society which took Pākehā domination and Māori subjection as a natural state. For the Māori, the relationship was necrotic as evidenced by language loss and cultural erosion.

In 1981, research by Benton[15] revealed that Māori language death was imminent, even though it was being taught in primary and secondary schools. Because of that stark revelation, organic leaders and intellectuals were forced to adopt the radical strategy of seceding from mainstream education. They took control of the education of their own children by setting up a parallel system of schooling. The immediate goal was to rescue the Māori language from extinction through kōhanga reo. These are language nests where pre-school education is conducted entirely in the Māori language. After four years of struggle to get them established, the Kōhanga Reo Trust was formed to receive state funding for the programme. The salient feature of the kōhanga reo movement, which started off as a language-recovery programme, is that it triggered the Māori dynamic of self-determination in education. There are today 700 kōhanga reo, which stand as testament to parental commitment to Māori identity, culture, and the education of their children.

Māori perception of the way education was used by the ruling class to subordinate them was stimulated at the Māori Educational Development Conference 1984. A paper by D. Hughes revealed the statistical manipulation of School Certificate marks by the examination board to give pass rates of over 80 percent for academic subjects and under 50 percent for non-academic subjects.[16] In the latter category were homecraft, metalwork, technical drawing and typing, the subjects to which the system tended to steer Māori students. Because of that tendency, the course options in most secondary schools locked the Māori language into the non-academic category. Few schools linked Māori with academic options. One year the pass rate in Māori language was as low as 39 percent. That revelation devastated Māori language teachers. They realised that they were working in a morally flawed system. It confirmed Māori in the view that the co-operative strategy with mainstream education had failed. Therefore, the only course was to secede and take over *in toto* the education of Māori children.

The philosophy of the kōhanga reo was extended to kura kaupapa Māori at the primary level. These are Māori-controlled schools which teach Māori values and the standard curriculum in the Māori language. They were started as parent initiatives at considerable personal cost to people with limited incomes. Once they were functional, they applied for state funding. There are at present fourteen such schools funded by the state. But they are insufficient to ensure language continuity from the kōhanga reo to primary school. There are fifty-five communities which have signalled their desire to start kura kaupapa. The leading protagonist of these schools is Dr Peter Sharples, who at the start of the 1993 academic year launched the first kura kaupapa secondary school. The long-term goal is to establish enough primary and secondary kura kaupapa to ensure Māori language continuity from pre-school through to university.

Tertiary education

In 1925, the Senate of the University of New Zealand was persuaded by Sir Apirana Ngata to introduce Māori language as a subject for the Bachelor of Arts degree. But it was not until 1951 that the first Māori studies course was offered at Auckland University. Fifteen years elapsed before Victoria University followed suit.[17] Since then, five other universities have come on stream with Māori studies departments. Two teacher training colleges began Māori studies courses in 1962. Eight years elapsed before the secondary teachers college, now the Auckland College of Education, followed suit. The polytechs were the last of the tertiary institutions to establish Māori studies departments.

The question arises, what is Māori studies? The way it sits at present in tertiary institutions, Māori studies can only be defined as being the study of Māori people, as if they were objects for scientific scrutiny. It is the study of Māori language, customs and traditions within the European conventions of organising and transmitting knowledge. Its genesis lay in the work of missionaries, administrators and amateur ethnographers. They expropriated and recorded Māori knowledge for their own purposes. The missionaries established an orthography of the language to promote conversion. The Governor and his administrators learned the Māori language and customs to gain control of land and resources. The ethnographer Percy Smith recorded Māori traditions but he violated the traditions by condensing and fitting them into European conceptions of history and linear time.

When Māori studies was introduced into university, the courses were designed to fit in with the curriculum and degree structure of the university. Māori people had little or no say in designing the curriculum of tertiary institutions. Nor did they have a say in the first appointments of Māori studies personnel at universities and other tertiary institutions. Consequently, the first Māori appointees tended to be conservative people who served as subalterns to the institutions of the state.

At their inception, Māori studies departments provided user-friendly environments for students who had no family tradition of tertiary education. In the 1950s, they were the first points of entry into university for the second wave of Māori graduates. These graduates then went on to staff the Māori studies departments in all the tertiary institutions. There are currently 6,000 Māori students enrolled in tertiary education. Although this is an improvement on thirty years ago, it should be double that number. What is encouraging is the spread of Māori students across all university departments and faculties. This development has been fostered by schools with limited enrolment such as medicine, science, law, and commerce recruiting Māori staff as role models, and allocating entry quota for Māori students.

Students who enrol in Māori studies do so primarily because they want to become fluent in Māori language and be of use in the development of their people. Within the constraints of the pedagogy of the university, it is not possible to teach oral fluency in language. For this reason, the university is one of the current sites of struggle for Māori emancipation and self-determination. The goal is empowerment of Māori to extend the principles underlying the kōhanga reo and kura kaupapa into the university system.

There are currently two models being pursued. The first model is Te Wānanga o Raukawa, a school of learning initiated by the Raukawa tribe, a few miles north of the capital city of Wellington. This tribal initiative, which started in 1981, was contemporaneous with the launch of the kōhanga reo movement. Its aim was to produce bicultural administrators, teachers and researchers who would enhance the quality of decision-making in the bureaucratic institutions of the nation.[18] Like the kōhanga reo, Te Wānanga o Raukawa was founded on voluntary service from qualified members of the tribe and private funds. The Raukawa trustees made four submissions to the Government to fund the institution between 1978 and 1981. They were rebuffed each time. But with the restructuring of the education system under Tomorrow's Schools, private providers of education, who can gain accreditation from the New Zealand Qualifications Authority as degree-granting institutions, qualify for government funding under the EFTS (Effective Full-Time Students) formula. Te Waananga o Raukawa went through the accreditation process in 1992. Its four degrees were approved for the 1993 academic year.

The second model is Te Whare Wānanga o Awanuia-rangi (The School of Learning of Awanuiarangi). This institution is named after the eponymous ancestor of Ngāti Awa in the Bay of Plenty. This school operates under the principle in Tomorrow's Schools of a 'university within a university'. It is an extension of the University of Waikato at Hamilton. It began in 1992 with a Diploma in Māori Health Studies and a Diploma in Māori Leadership.

The Māori Studies Department at Auckland University was restructured in 1993 in terms of the second model. It took the initial step in April this year by constituting itself as Te Wānanga o Waipapa. The immediate goal of the Wānanga is to mount a credible undergraduate and post-graduate programme that is relevant to Māori needs. That includes fluency in the language and iwi development. For its degrees to be credible, the Wānanga will define its own theoretical framework derived from Te Ao Māori, the Māori way of knowing and responding to the phenomenological world. The comprehensible paradigm is whakapapa, which defines the creation of the universe, genesis of the gods and the descent of human beings. A dynamic theory would incorporate the indigenous concept of the past and present as a single reality that will inform the future, in the struggle for the assertion of Māori sovereignty.

29 May 1993
(Paper delivered to First Nations Conference on Higher Education, Anchorage, Alaska)

10: SCIENCE, INTELLECTUAL PROPERTY AND CULTURAL SAFETY

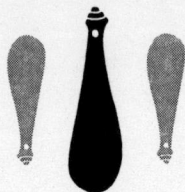

Māori medicine

IN RECENT years there has been a revival of interest in Māori medicine and a genuine attempt to incorporate it alongside orthodox medicine. Unfortunately, Māori medicine is little understood, so that there is a danger with the present cultural revival taking place that Māori medical practice might be expected to deliver more than it promises.

The pre-European Māori did not have a germ theory of medicine. Indeed, if Houghton's *The First New Zealanders* is correct, it would seem they had no germs at all. Contagious diseases such as chicken-pox, measles and influenza were unknown. This is because they need a population of 50,000 to transmit and sustain them. When the ancestors of the Polynesians began ocean-going voyages from New Britain around 1500 B.C. and spread into the Polynesian islands over the next 2,000 years, germs were filtered out en route.

Yet despite that fortuitous outcome, the Māori had a life-expectancy of thirty years because of their harsh life. Teeth were ground down to the pulp cavity by their gritty diet, jaws became abscessed, teeth fell out, nutrition suffered and the severe winters finished them off. Anyone who survived to forty was a kaumātua.

The literature on Māori medicine is rather sparse.

Captain Cook and Dieffenbach of the New Zealand Company both recorded the use of steam rising from heated leaves for medicinal purposes. John Rutherford, an English sailor who lived among Māori from 1816 to 1826, attested to the Māori ability to heal battle wounds by the application of herbal remedies. Te Rangihīroa (*The Coming of the Maori*) described the Māori treatment of ailments 'obvious to the sight'. These included warts, boils, toothache, and the use of heat to relieve pains after birth or difficult menstruation. The practice of blood-letting to relieve pain was also used. The traditions of tribal warfare recorded the application of crude first-aid to battle wounds. One of the most famous battle wounds was the split skull of the Arawa ancestor Rangitihi. Rangitihi bound his head with vines and continued fighting. This event is eulogised in the Arawa aphorism, 'Rangitihi's is the head to be marvelled at.'

While the literature records the treatment of external ailments, it has little to say on the treatment of internal indispositions. It would appear the use of oral medication was copied from the missionaries. Once missionaries were seen testing native plants for their medicinal properties, the practice was readily adopted by the Māori. They experimented for themselves and developed over 200 plant and herbal remedies. This post-European development was abandoned in the last fifty years in favour of Pākehā medicines. Few Māori today would brave the bitter taste of flax water as a cure for constipation ahead of the modern patent laxatives.

The main focus of Māori medical practice was psychosomatic and spiritual healing. There are stories in traditions of bodily processes being afflicted by mental states. The most celebrated of these pertained to the birth of Tūtānekai. His mother Rangiuru went into protracted labour. In the end the midwives called in the tohunga who recited karakia of the most potent kind to facilitate the birth. When that failed, he taxed Rangiuru with having committed a hara (indiscretion), whereupon she confessed that her husband was not the father of her child. It was Tūwharetoa.

The tohunga recited his incantations again and in the

appropriate place in the child's genealogy he inserted the name Tūwharetoa. The child was then delivered with ease. The case of Tūtānekai's birth is in modern parlance an example of a psychosomatic disorder for which Māori medical practice had an adequate technique – they knew confession was good for the soul.

The main theory of Māori medicine was metaphysical or spiritual healing. According to this theory, when an individual became ill and there was no apparent physical cause then it was spiritually caused. The theory rested on the belief in mate Māori (Māori illness), which was distinct from Pākehā diseases. It was thought that if the laws of tapu were transgressed then the gods withdrew their protection from the mauri (life force) of an individual. His or her body would become ill and in severe cases end in death. The cure was spiritual healing. This involved withdrawal from normal activities, karakia and bathing in sacred waters. Special puna (springs) were set aside for this purpose.

Another form of mate Māori was mākutu (sorcery). Usually a mākutu was performed by an opponent out for utu for a real or imagined offence. The target of mākutu was the mauri. But its effectiveness was enhanced if a sign was given to the victim that a mākutu had been put on him. On coming across the sign, which might be a post with a piece of maro (loin cloth) attached or a bunch of grass, the victim's mauri was startled. His heart would heave and his pulse race as the adrenalin pumped by fear of the unknown poured into his blood-stream. Loss of appetite, physical decline and death would ensue unless a tohunga ahurewa (high priest) was called in to counter the mākutu.

There are as many causes of mate Māori as there are human fears. These fears and their manifestations as mate Māori are derived from tikanga Māori (Māori culture) and are the province of the faith-healing tohunga rather than the physician. In cross-cultural analysis, Māori medicine has a place as a branch of psychiatry. To elevate it beyond that is to indulge in myth-making.

10 November 1986
(*Listener*)

Intellectual property

THE INTERNATIONAL Year of Indigenous People has come and gone, but the problems that confront some indigenous people around the world have hardly changed because of it. For this reason, the Nobel prize-winner Rigoberta Menchu proposed at a conference in Norway that there should be an International Decade of Indigenous People. Menchu, more than anyone else in the world, knows that such a timeframe is needed to bring the plight of Amerindians in Latin America to the attention of the international community. She thinks that the concerted moral persuasion of the people of the world would be helpful in deterring repressive regimes from genocidal practices.

Last year, Menchu had a gruelling schedule of speaking engagements around the world as UN Ambassador for the Year of Indigenous People. She even made it to New Zealand where she was given a formal Māori welcome at Ōrākei Marae. Menchu speaks passionately about military repression in Guatemala. Although the indigenous people, known collectively as the Maya, constitute a majority of 75 percent of the population, they live in fear of the Ladino minority and their military power. The Maya of Guatemala are a nation without a state. They have no political rights, no rights to land, no rights to free association and freedom of speech, and no rights to maintain their Indian language and culture.

The violence of the military regime against the indigenous people of Guatemala is linked to discoveries of oil, nickel and uranium. Guatemala has the potential to be the third-largest producer of oil in Central America after Mexico and Venezuela. The Government, which is the political arm of stockbrokers, bankers and businessmen, simply expropriated the mineral resources and brought in transnational companies to exploit them. Indians in the way of development were terrorised by paramilitary death squads, which perpetrated extra-judicial killings. The death squads targeted campesino co-operatives and trade unions, which they alleged were subversive communist organisations. The death squads enabled the Government to distance itself from the political killings, which were described in official communiques as being committed by 'heavily armed', 'civilian dressed', 'unidentified people'.

Refugees from military terror escape across the border to Mexico. Stragglers are rounded up and confined by the military to model villages, a sanitised term for concentration camps. Most of the model villages are located in remote rural areas. Show-place model villages, for the gaze of inter-national aid agencies, are located near arterial routes such as the Pan-American Highway.

Despite having democratic elections under United Nations supervision in 1984, the indigenous people of Guatemala remain oppressed because the elections were fraudulent. Rigoberta Menchu's mission in life is to speak out against the oppression of her people.

Apart from Menchu's fleeting visit, there was one other notable event precipitated in New Zealand by the Inter-national Year of Indigenous People. The Mataatua tribes of the Bay of Plenty hosted the first International Conference on the Intellectual Property Rights of Indigenous People. Such a conference is overdue.

Māori people have had a long and deep-seated aversion to the commodification of their knowledge, particularly when information given freely ends up in book form and provides royalties for the author. Sir George Grey, for instance, collected the Māori creation myths and published them in both Māori and English. He did this without acknowledging the Rangiwewehi chief Te Rangikaheke as their source. By the time John White was commissioned by the Government to write *The Ancient History of the Māori*, published in 1887, attitudes had changed. White paid his informants one pound to write down their stories in notebooks. A half-filled book merited only ten shillings. Consequently, some informants stretched their imagination to earn the full pound. For this reason, some of White's information is of dubious merit. Although fabrication was motivated by cupidity, it was also a way of taking the mickey out of powerful Pākehā more interested in self-aggrandisement than the well-being of a subject people.

By the turn of the century, commodification of Māori knowledge had reached a point where Māori informants were not above hoaxing Pākehā authors as a way of getting back at an exploitive relationship. One of the most celebrated was Ettie Rout, whose book *Māori Symbolism* is a monument to the naivety of amateur ethnographers. The book chronicles the customs, science, and hygiene and sexual practices of the Māori. All pretty weird stuff, which becomes intelligible only when you look at the name of Rout's informant. He called himself Te Rake, a name that translates into English as The Rake, which he probably was. This is another example of Māori turning the tables on a cultural voyeur.

In our own time, Michael King, who wrote an excellent biography of Te Puea, has been much criticised by Māori activists for writing books on Māori subjects. Being sensitive to the nuances of the post-modern world, King ceased writing in the Māori field. The gagging of King was in effect a crude *de facto* application of the notion of intellectual property and its control by the owners.

Now, the Mataatua tribes have codified their thoughts on the protection of intellectual and cultural property rights of indigenous people. They want those rights protected by national law and incorporated into the proposed United Nations convention on the rights of indigenous people. In the meantime, with the advent of 'virtual reality' in electronic media, the tribes have to initiate their own protective measures.

Professor Hermann Maurer, of Auckland University, warns that Māori leaders might be gulled into selling the exclusive electronic rights to ancestral treasures, such as a meeting house, to an overseas company. Photographing and videoing the art work of a meeting house or cultural performances on a marae for $50,000 might appear to be a good deal. Maurer argues that the electronic copyright, whereby the original can be reproduced many times over is, in effect, a licence to print money in the future.

15 January 1994
(*Metro*)

'We're back'

THE CULTURAL renaissance of the Māori, which had its genesis in the work of Sir Apirana Ngata at the turn of the century, has flourished in our own time to the extent that there is a widespread movement in the recovery of indigenous knowledge. That recovery of knowledge from the trauma of the colonial experience is being promoted on marae, in independent tribal schools of learning, and in universities.

Besides the standard Māori language and culture papers at university, degree papers are now offered in Māori geography, law, education, psychology and indigenous science. This inclusion of Māori knowledge is a remarkable reversal of the policy of exclusion, and even suppression, under the Tohunga Suppression Act 1907.

The early manifestations of the recovery of suppressed knowledge occurred in the domain of carving and the interior decoration of houses. Carving had all but died out at the turn of the century because of missionary condemnation of 'ancestor worship' and the overt depiction of human sexuality in the carving of male and female genitals. Missionaries, and occasionally curators of museums, hacked off ancestral penises in the interest of civilisation. The outcome of this symbolic emasculation of Māori culture was the replacement of carving by painted ancestors in houses built at the turn of the century.

The school of carving established in 1928 by Ngata at Rotorua reversed the death of a culture as exemplified by the visual arts. As the population recovered from the brink of extinction, Māori confidence was reflected in their art. Penises are now carved larger than life, an overt, symbolic gesture proclaiming 'We're back'. Although most people are capable of interpreting art as a reflection of the human condition, there is a minority stuck in a sexual time warp. Last month, when the Governor-General, Dame Catherine Tizard, opened the Auckland Regional Council's Aratiki Visitors' Centre in the Waitakere Ranges, five people objected to the genital details of the 11-metre carving. One Judith Lambert, of Glenfield, condemned them as pornographic. But on the matter of the statue at the entrance to the Domain by the Auckland Hospital there has been a deafening silence. Perhaps Lambert's objection is confined only to black penises.

The other symbolic manifestation of cultural recovery was the waka project of 1990, and its precurser *Hawaikinui*. This double-hulled waka built by Te Matahi Whakataka, and sailed to New Zealand from Tahiti in 1985, retraced the ancestral route of the waka that colonised New Zealand late in the first millennium. Landfall was accomplished by 'Te ara whetū', the star path of celestial navigation. The reverse journey to Rarotonga was made by Hec Busby on *Aureretanga* in 1992.

Moved by these feats of recovery of empirical knowledge in the arts, and in the science of celestial navigation, Māori academics have joined the cultural renaissance by incorporating Māori knowledge into their teaching programmes. The validation and incorporation of Māori knowledge in the curriculum of educational institutions has not been accomplished without resistance from some Pākehā who are out of tune with post-modernism. The media fuss over 'cultural safety' in nurse training at Christchurch Polytech last year, and more recently at Hamilton Polytech, are examples. People with closed minds see Māori knowledge as different, they feel threatened, and put up road-blocks to exclude it. The most recent exponent of this line of thought is Mike Dickison, a researcher at Victoria University. Dickison denies that Māori were capable of scientific thought and the application of the scientific method.

Western science grew out of the positivist view that the world of reality can be understood by the objective observation of the facts to establish connections or causal relations between them. This mode of thought is not peculiar to the West.

Polynesian navigators in the Marquesas, the Society Islands, and the Cook Islands observed the annual migration of flocks of sooty shearwaters, godwits and cuckoos to the southwest. From that observation they generated the hypothesis of the existence of a new land waiting to be discovered. To do the job, Polynesians invented the fastest sailing ships in the world, the double-hulled waka, precursor of the modern catamaran.

Polynesians also developed their own science of celestial navigation. They divided the horizon into thirty-two points and used horizon stars to steer a course to the new land. When the land was discovered, zenith stars standing over the island at midnight helped fix its latitude. Return voyages relayed the information back to home islands. This enabled others to replicate the feat and bring about multiple settlement of New Zealand.

The first settlers encountered difficulties in establishing the kūmara in the colder climate of New Zealand. Kūmara does not normally grow beyond 30 degrees north or south of the equator. Even in the northernmost part of New Zealand, the growing season was too short for the kūmara to flower and produce seeds.

These problems were resolved by a number of scientific solutions. In the absence of seeds, the settlers resorted to shoot propagation. They developed a 'hot-box' lined with straw to promote early shooting of the tubers. When the danger of frost had passed, the shoots were planted in specially prepared mounds. The growing range was pushed progressively southward by making use of radiant heat from stone walls and stones embedded in the cultivations. The gravel pits in Nelson attest to the use of gravel to enhance the growing conditions of the kūmara in the South Island.

The problem of keeping the tubers over the winter months was resolved by controlled temperature storage at 15–17 degrees centigrade in underground pits lined with bracken. This suppressed knowledge is now being taught in universities, and denial of its existence by the Dickisons of this world will not wish it away.

30 May 1994
(*Metro*)

Cultural safety

IN RECENT months, I have chaired hearings for the New Zealand Qualifications Authority on applications for approval of Bachelor of Nursing degrees from two polytechnic institutions. In addition to the standard curriculum of nursing practice and clinical training, both applications had small sections on 'cultural safety'. This is a recent innovation in nurse training. Cultural safety is a generic term embracing all cultures. But because it included a section on Māori culture and Treaty issues, I warned one of the applicants it was likely to meet opposition. For this reason they needed to marshal their arguments for its inclusion, as exclusion of Māori concerns from the curriculum has been the dominant practice for more than a century.

Within weeks of that warning, cultural safety came under fire in the media as a consequence of the claims of Anna Penn that she had been done in by this new subject. For weeks, the polemics and rhetoric raged in the media, and continue today in letters to the editors of our daily papers.

An editorial in the *Christchurch Press* likened cultural safety to 'an instrument of tyranny', a form of 'social engineering' to ensure that nurse trainees conformed to 'politically correct' and sensitive patterns of 'thought, speech and deed'. A commentary in the *Mail* by Glyn Clayton dubbed the issue one of 'tribal extremism'. Although the *Press* grudgingly admitted that the cultural safety component of nurse training at Christchurch Polytechnic comprised only 104 hours (i.e. 3.5 percent) of a 3,000-hour course, it continued the polemics without doing its homework.

Instead of defining cultural safety for the edification of its readers, the *Press* continued the attack by arguing that it carried undue weight in the curriculum. It cited David Wills, national director of the Nurses Society, who claimed that New Zealand was producing culturally safe nurses who were lacking in basic clinical skills. In support of this assertion, Wills implied cultural safety diminished clinical training because it comprised 20 percent of state final examinations. The claim is outrageous, because there is continuous on-course assessment of clinical training and nursing practice throughout the three-year degree course.

In view of the heat generated by the controversy over cultural safety, I decided to investigate the subject for myself to see if its meaning was the same for me as for those who propounded it.

The first visionary of trans-cultural nursing practice was Madeline Leininger, of the United States. In the 1950s, Leininger developed her vision of transcending Anglo-American culture in the delivery of nursing care to people of other cultures in America. Over the next twenty years, Leininger published books and papers where she defined her theories and concepts of trans-cultural nursing and the blending of two worlds. These theories were incorporated into nurse-training programmes in a number of universities in the United States.

In New Zealand, the visionary who followed in the footsteps of Leininger is Irihāpeti Ramsden. She is the author of the concept of whakaruruhau, cultural safety in nursing practice. Ramsden, like other creative thinkers, took on board the work of her predecessors, such as Leininger, and remodelled it to fit the New Zealand scene. Ramsden argues that trans-cultural nursing assumes an external observer position. It teaches nurses to observe people in terms of a checklist from a multi-cultural smorgasbord. The model is deficient for dealing with diversity within cultures, such as differences between liberals and conservatives, young and old, urban and rural, rich and poor, and gender interaction.

Ramsden contends that all nursing interactions are bicultural, because interaction can be with only one person at a time. There is one giver of the message and one receiver, regardless of the numbers of people and cultural frameworks. She argues that the trans-cultural model of nursing is also deficient in not requiring nurses to examine their own cultural realities, namely how their attitudes and behaviours impinge on others. Because the nurse is also a bearer of culture, which has hitherto been taken for granted, the nurse is now the focus of training in cultural safety.

In 1989, Ramsden was the first Māori appointed to the Education Committee of the New Zealand Nursing Council. The following year, she was commissioned by all but one of the heads of nurse-training schools to write a report on cultural safety in nurse education. Ramsden held hui with Māori health organisations and health workers in four Regional Health Authorities. These hui chose the term whakaruruhau, cultural safety, ahead of 'culturally appropriate' for this new element in nurse training.

The aim of cultural safety is to educate nurses to examine their own cultural realities, so that with self-knowledge they can be more flexible and open-minded in the delivery of service to people from other cultures. Although there is a bicultural Māori-Pākehā component in cultural safety training, the principles learned in this section of the course are applicable to all cultures. A subsidiary aim is to produce educated nurses who will not blame victims of historic processes for their current plight of poor health. The cardinal values of cultural safety training are sensitivity, awareness, and safe nursing practice with people of all cultures.

Ramsden argues that cultural safety is about improving life-chances, through better access to health services rather than ethnography. Approximately 40 percent of the course should cover historical and social issues that relate to nursing and midwifery. Pākehā culture should take up 30 percent of the course, with the other 30 percent devoted to Māori traditions, customs and preparation for visits to marae. Visits to marae should take place late in the second year, otherwise, without adequate preparation, negative responses are likely to be elicited from students who feel threatened by a situation where they are not in control. That of course is where Anna Penn, who triggered this whole debate, came in. She did not attend the preparatory hui, behaved in an inappropriate manner, and was judged by the Christchurch Polytech to be not culturally safe.

30 August 1993
(*Metro*)

Whakaruruhau

HISTORICALLY, education has been touted as an objective and politically neutral enterprise, teaching a universal corpus of knowledge that transcends race, class, and cultural boundaries. This ideological packaging of eduction is rarely questioned by its consumers, who see education as the passport to a better future.

In recent times, the apolitical presentation of education has been interrogated by neo-Marxists and critical theorists. They argue that education is deeply involved in the politics of culture. The construction of the curriculum has long been implicated in the conflicts of race, class, gender and religion. The elites who run the system decide what constitutes knowledge, and whose knowledge is validated for inclusion in the curriculum.

Māori do not have to be Marxists or critical theorists to know these elementary truths about the nature of the education system. For more than a century, their language was actively suppressed in schools. The conflict engendered two strategic responses. The first sought to make schooling more user-friendly by modifying the curriculum to include Māori knowledge. The second strategy was for Māori to take control of their own education by establishing kōhanga reo, kura kaupapa, and wānanga. But since Māori cannot replicate an entire education system, there are many areas where they have to resort to the co-operative strategy of seeking inclusion within existing training provisions. One of the most controversial of these at the moment is kawa whakaruruhau, otherwise known as cultural safety, in nurse training.

In June, Melanie Davis, a Young National, launched her political ambitions at a party conference in an attack on cultural safety. The fuss she made precipitated an inquiry by a parliamentary select committee. The committee will examine student claims that too much emphasis is placed on Māori culture, thereby openly enmeshing education as a site of struggle in the politics of culture. Few people understand what is meant by cultural safety, and are readily misled by superficial claims that it means too much Māori culture in nurse training.

Cultural safety is actually an inadequate rendering of a Māori cultural metaphor. The original metaphor refers to the giant podocarps of the forest, as tōtara whakaruruhau, the sheltering, nurturing wind-break of the great forest of Tāne. The mighty kauri is also interchangeable with tōtara in the metaphor. This figure of speech is heard most often in eulogies to the dead, likening their passing to the fall of the sheltering giants of the forest. In this context the metaphor takes on spiritual connotations, as the decaying tree provides nourishment for the saplings it sheltered. The term kawa, which replaces tree in the metaphor, means protocol. Although the concept of a nurturing protocol is quite apt for the nursing profession, few people know what it means. But because of the negative political connotations now attached to the term cultural safety, I shall use the term whakaruruhau.

A nursing degree requires 3,000 hours to complete. Of that time, only 3.5 percent is spent on whakaruruhau. That 3.5 percent is divided between Pākehā culture, 1 percent, Māori culture 1 percent, and social issues arising out of New Zealand's colonial history 1.5 percent. The rationale for this arrangement of the whakaruruhau curriculum is that Māori and Pākehā constitute binary opposites that mutually define each other as the founding elements of the nation state.

What started off as a hopeful partnership of two disparate cultures in the brave new world under the Treaty of Waitangi soured as soon as Pākehā gained numerical superiority. The trauma of colonisation, loss of land, status, and identity brought on a state of dis-ease among Māori. One of its most pervasive features was a crippling sense of whakamā, the shame of the underclass, an incapacity to act decisively in a world not of their making. Associated symptoms of Māori dis-ease include alcoholism, poor health, low life-expectancy, poor educational performance and high unemployment. On the other hand, Māori were not passive victims. They struggled to recover their lost humanity, and that struggle has become increasingly manifest in our own time as a cultural renaissance, a pride in Māori identity and achievement. But despite that resurgence of Māori pride, the dis-ease of the negative statistics remains.

The purpose of kawa whakaruruhau is to study the genesis of these negative social indices for Māori and the barriers against improvement. That is why Pākehā culture is studied. It is the flip-side of the coin which hitherto has not been interrogated for its part in the production of Māori dis-ease. The reason for this cultural exculpation is the tacit assumption that Pākehā culture is the norm, the yardstick of goodness and enlightenment by which everything else in the little universe of New Zealand is measured.

Because Māori occupy the moral high ground of our past, it is uncomfortable for Pākehā to confront our colonial history. It is disconcerting to learn that the native school curriculum was designed to train Māori as the labouring underclass. For those in the nursing profession, it is disconcerting to learn that Māori were first admitted to nurse training provided they practised only among their own people. Educational authorities went so far as to advise Hospital Boards not to employ trained Māori nurses. Although Māori health statistics were appalling, the authorities became concerned only if Māori diseases were a threat to the health of the Pākehā populace. Māori nurses had to be mentally tough to survive ingrained racial attitudes that characterised them as lacking in application, reliability, and powers of concentration to pass exams. They were even subjected to sleeping in segregated quarters.

Whakaruruhau is about dealing with the residues of this colonial baggage of domination and subordination in nurse training. It is not about Māori culture *per se*, but the delivery of effective health care to all consumers as equals.

28 August 1995
(*Metro*)

11: IMMIGRATION

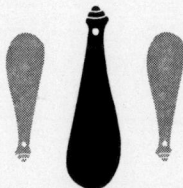

The Government's economic mantra of BIP immigration

THE TREATY of Waitangi signed in 1840 brought into being the nation state of New Zealand. It is the charter for constitutional government in the country. The signatories were Captain William Hobson on behalf of the British Crown, and 540 chiefs of the land on behalf of their respective tribes.[1] In the first clause of the treaty, the chiefs ceded kāwanatanga to the Crown. They understood kāwanatanga to mean the establishment of government, laws, and a judicial system.

Under the second clause of the Treaty, the Crown guaranteed tino rangatiratanga, the absolute chieftainship of the chiefs over their lands, homes and treasured possessions. The guarantee of chieftainship was in effect a guarantee of mana. The chiefs understood this to mean the confirmation of their sovereign rights in return for a limited concession of kāwanatanga.[2] The Waitangi Tribunal interpreted kāwanatanga and tino rangatiratanga as two equally balanced principles with the observation that 'the Māori retained his mana without denying that of the Queen'.[3]

With the advance of colonisation, the balance between kāwanatanga and tino rangatiratanga was overridden by the settler Government. Between 1854 and 1867, when Māori were excluded from Parliament, the Government made war on the Māori and passed laws to expropriate their land, forests and fisheries. In our own time, these and subsequent actions of past governments right up to the present day have been challenged by Māori leaders before the Waitangi Tribunal and in the High Court. The findings of both these bodies are steps along the way to restoring the principle of tino rangatiratanga towards parity with kāwanatanga.

The ruling of Justice Greig in the High Court in October 1987, that the ITQ fisheries management system breached Māori fishing rights, introduced the word partnership into the contemporary discourse on the Treaty. He ordered an interim stop to the issue of Individual Transferable Quota for designated species of fish and advised the Government to negotiate with its Treaty partner for the recognition and use of those rights.[4] Despite that advice, the concept of partnership in the business of government is still embryonic and therefore easily overlooked or deliberately overridden. The most recent example of failure to consult the Māori Treaty partner is the present Government's immigration policy, which aims to bring in 20,000 immigrants per annum.

The original charter for immigration into New Zealand is in the preamble of the Treaty of Waitangi. There it states that Her Majesty Queen Victoria of the United Kingdom

> has deemed it necessary, in consequence of the great number of Her Majesty's subjects who have already settled in New Zealand, and the rapid extension of emigration from both Europe and Australia which is still in progress, to constitute and appoint a functionary properly authorised to treat with the Aborigines of New Zealand for the recognition of her Majesty's sovereign authority over the whole or any part of those islands.[5]

The present generation of Māori leaders abides by the agreement of their ancestors to allow immigration into New Zealand from the countries nominated in the preamble of the Treaty, namely Europe, Australia and the United Kingdom. But, for any variation of that agreement to be validated, they expect the Government to consult them as the descendants of the Māori Treaty partner. The Human Rights Commission endorsed that position with its recommendation to the Government that the Treaty of Waitangi should be considered in any decisions on immigration policy.[6]

The Commission's advice, however, was not properly heeded. Mr Birch, the Minister of Immigration, called meetings with thirteen selected Māori leaders in Auckland and fourteen in Wellington after the working party on immigration delivered its report. The purpose of the meetings was to gain Māori acquiescence to the recommendations of the report. Although many speakers spoke against the immigration proposals, the minister, in response to a question in the House, listed all those in attendance as being 'broadly positive' towards his immigration scheme.[7] This glossing-over of Māori opposition is consistent with the procedure of elites generating policy from above and imposing it on the people below. The report was a *fait accompli*, and the minister's restricted discourse with Māori leaders after the fact gave an illusion of democratic consultation.

Derivation of the business immigration policy

The present 'skills' and Business Immigration Policy is derived from the monetarist policies of both the Labour and National parties and the Business Roundtable. Although the primary agenda was an economic solution to New Zealand's stagnant economy, there is also an underlying subsidiary agenda of disempowering Māori by flooding the country with new immigrants from Asia and other countries.

As soon as it came to power in 1984, the Labour Government began the process of reviewing New Zealand's immigration policy with a view to changing immigration laws. The determination of policy was influenced by the counter-hegemonic struggle of the Māori against the state, the Māori ideology of biculturalism and the need to legitimate the Pākehā presence in New Zealand. This subsidiary agenda is made explicit in the 1986 review of immigration policy by the Minister of Immigration, Kerry Burke.

The review asserts that New Zealand is a country of immigrants, including the Māori, despite their prior right of discovery and millennial association with the land. Defining the Māori as immigrants negates their status as tāngata whenua, and lumps them in with the Pākehā immigrants who took over the country, and later immigrants from the Pacific rim.[8] The review disguises the monocultural and Euro-centric control over the governing institutions of the country by claiming that immigration has moulded its national character as a Pacific country.[9] That character is then identified as multiculturalism, which is a direct negation of the Māori ideology of biculturalism.

The aim of the new immigration policy is to 'enrich the multicultural fabric of New Zealand society through the selection of new settlers, principally on the strength of their potential personal contribution to the future well-being of New Zealand'.[10] Selection on occupational grounds is based on an occupational priority list (which has since been scrapped) and skilled jobs which cannot be filled internally.

The review defines a sub-category of economic migration as 'entrepreneur immigration', which is expected to create employment for others.[11] In the seven years that entrepreneur immigration was in operation, 225 business immigrants from Germany, Hong Kong, the United Kingdom and the United States brought in capital amounting to $106,866,000. Although the review comments that this is a 'useful result', it admitted that this was not a significant element in the total immigrant inflow or the nation's economic development.[12] Despite that admission, the review advocated promoting business immigration by selecting people (with entrepreneurial skills) rather than proposals and setting a figure of $150,000 to meet housing, living and establishment costs for the first year.

The National Party election manifesto advocated a positive immigration policy. It cited the Poot Report in support of the present scheme to bring in 20,000 immigrants per annum. Poot and associates assert that New Zealand's standard of living can be maintained only under 'high levels of immigration when the associated expansion of the economy generates productivity improvements through technical change and economies of scale'.[13]

Another advocate of immigration's role in creating an economy of scale is Douglas Myers, vice-chairman of the Business Roundtable, who is headlined in the *People's Voice* wanting an Asian-type labour market in New Zealand. Myer asserted that freeing up the labour market would generate high profits from high growth and efficiency.[14]

The Business Roundtable commissioned Wolfgang Kaspar, Professor of Economics at the University College (Australian Defence Academy) of the University of New South Wales, to make a case for a business immigration scheme. The report, entitled *Populate or Languish*, was produced in July 1990. Kaspar makes a number of assertions in favour of a proactive immigration policy without adducing any evidence for the benefits claimed. For instance:

> Market principles suggest that immigration in a competitive economy increases output and improves productivity.[15] (Quoted from U.S. Congress Economic Report of the President, 1986.)

> If migration is open to all-comers, including the desperate pyramid climbers, more competition-minded migrants will self-select.[16]

> Immigrants may often work as catalysts for change in static industries.[17]

Kaspar asserts that America's 'melting-pot' has been highly successful in generating economic wealth[18] but this is grossly misleading. It ignores the expropriation of Red Indians' land and mineral resources, which were the foundation of American wealth. It also ignores the draining of wealth out of Central America by the United Fruit Company.

Kaspar's suggestion that immigrant Mexicans in California organise relationships with their employers differently because they see striking as a waste of production and a loss of income is also misleading. Kaspar makes no mention of the historic struggle of the Chicano hero Chavez to improve the working conditions of so-called 'wetbacks', the illegal immigrant workers who were shamelessly exploited in the orchards and gardens of the San Joaquin Valley. That struggle was recorded in graffiti throughout the horticultural region of California. Its most stunning memento, which can still be seen today, is a mural on the pylons of an overbridge in San Diego depicting Chavez's struggle.

Paulo Freire defines oppression as 'any situation in which A objectively exploits B or hinders his pursuit of self-affirmation'.[19] The oppressed, says Freire, 'as objects or "things", have no purposes except those that their oppressors prescribe for them'.[20] In the case of migrant workers, they are defined merely as a source of cheap labour and profits for employers. It is unconscionable for an academic such as Kaspar to advocate the admission of migrant workers, who, because of their political weakness, have no choice but to organise their relationship with employers 'differently' to the point of becoming victims of exploitation. The gain to the employer from an exploitive regime is only temporary, as the oppressed will inevitably organise, as did Chavez and his followers, to improve their conditions of employment.

The uncritical acceptance by Kaspar of a statement quoted from J. L. Simon that the crucial capital nowadays is 'human capital'[21] is disturbing. It reduces humans to the level of economic work units, whose *raison d'être* is to increase capital in the economic system. This reduction of humans to capital units is dehumanising and fosters unprincipled and predatory attitudes to people around the world. Kaspar exemplifies this exploitative ethic when he says New Zealand 'has the opportunity to attract a crucial production factor [meaning immigrants], to launch faster economic growth . . . there is a growing number of young adults with a good education who live in Third World countries'.[22] The question of what effect recruitment of such people would have on the development of their own countries is not considered.

Although New Zealand might be seen to be an attractive place to immigrants because of its political stability, moderate climate, excellent natural environment, low taxation, cheap housing, high moral standards, and good education and welfare system, Kaspar thinks these assets are not enough to attract immigrants. He cites poor economic growth, poor labour relations, unreliability of suppliers and concern over racial harmony as disincentives.[23]

Kaspar argues that 'man-made' interventions enhance the attractiveness of a country to capital, skills and entrepreneurs. These include tax laws encouraging business, regulations affecting labour costs and flexibility of work practices.[24] To this end, we see corporations exhorting the Government to 'identify winners' and back them by doing away with the 'level playing field', and the Government bringing in the Employment Contracts Act. The intent of the latter measure is to lower the wage structure of New Zealand labour in order to attract trans-national corporations to relocate in New Zealand, as they have done in Taiwan and Korea. But this policy does not take into account the fact that New Zealand is a primary-producing country, is resource-poor in terms of minerals and oil, and is the most distant country from world markets. It is difficult to produce competitively priced manufactured goods with high freight costs on top of manufacturing costs.

Despite the flaws in the argument that a proactive immigration policy will resolve New Zealand's economic problems, and the lack of evidence that it will do so, immigration is put forward as the answer. Kasper concludes:

> If immigration is to be a means of breaking with a stagnant past, sizeable migrant numbers should be admitted . . . With an annual intake of 30–40,000, and an annual population growth rate of 1.7 percent between now and the year 2021, the New Zealand population would then reach six million.[25]

If Kaspar's suggestion is implemented, the population would be two million above the projected four million from natural increase. The doubling of New Zealand's population in a mere thirty years by a 'man-made' intervention has serious implications for environmental degradation, education, welfare, the increased consumption of our own primary produce, and for the tāngata whenua. With unemployment predicted by Berl to rise to 200,000, accompanied by cuts in unemployment and welfare benefits, it is abundantly clear that the Government is not capable of looking after the three million people we have now. It does not make sense to bring in more people to exacerbate the problems we already have.

With few exceptions, most Māori would reject Kaspar's soothsaying that they should not fear becoming a smaller minority in a situation where land and resources would be 'competed away'. Like Job's comforter, he says, 'They [Māori] could instead live in a nation of many minorities where the Māori minority fitted in much better as an equal social group.'[26]

Kaspar's view is advanced with the ignorant naivety of the outsider who knows nothing of the 150-year struggle of the Māori against an unjust colonial regime. The reduction of the Māori to a position of one of many minorities negates their status as tāngata whenua and will enable the Government to neutralise their claims for justice under the Treaty of Waitangi even more effectively than it does now. For this reason, the ideology of multiculturalism as a rationale for immigration must be rejected. In addition to its economic rationale, the Government's immigration policy must be seen for what it is, a strategy to suppress the counter-hegemonic struggle of the Māori.

The Business Roundtable, which commissioned the Kaspar report, raised queries over the use of abundant 'free goods', including clean air, water resources, wilderness areas and other collectively owned assets. The Roundtable argued that the ill-defined ownership of some of these assets weakens the incentive to use them well, to strike a balance between conservation and development, to achieve socially desirable trade-offs between competing uses. To this end, the Roundtable wants resource management reforms aimed at clarifying property rights.

The ownership and use of the assets referred to by the Roundtable is precisely what Māori have challenged in recent years before the Waitangi Tribunal. The Kaituna and Manukau claims over the water of the Kaituna and Waikato rivers are cases in point. The Māori fisheries claim in the

High Court is another. These are examples of Māori claims standing in the way of local body and corporate business plans for development based on the use of those resources. Measures to accommodate Roundtable concerns in impending resource management law reform is likely to generate further claims, particularly in view of the Government's power to sell licences to business interests for development projects along New Zealand's coastline.

Working party on immigration

Following the Kaspar report, Mr Birch, the Minister of Immigration, appointed a working party on immigration in December 1990. It consisted of three members. The Māori Treaty partner was not represented on the working party. Neither were women. The role of the working party was to decide how to implement a dynamic Business Immigration Policy incorporating supervision of investments, and an appraisal process for a 'skilled occupational migrants' programme. Examining the role of immigrant consultants, and advising on a system of accreditation, was also in the brief.[27]

The working party did not question the Government's premise that there was a need to attract business and qualified immigrants in substantial numbers for the economic development of New Zealand. Nor did the working party attempt to substantiate the need itself. It was accepted as an article of faith, which, if repeated often enough like a mantra, would become a reality.

The working party's report was delivered to the minister in March 1991. It warned that, since New Zealand was competing with Canada and Australia as the preferred destinations of quality migrants, appropriate policies promoting New Zealand as a destination would have to be put into place.

The Immigration Act 1987 provides the legislative framework for the admission of immigrants under the economic, social and humanitarian streams for permanent entry. In the economic stream are occupational and Business Immigration

Policy sub-groups. The occupational sub-group aims to facilitate entry of skilled immigrants to fill gaps in New Zealand's labour market. Those gaps are not defined. Employers are simply required to demonstrate that a position cannot be filled from the local labour market, whereupon they are allowed to recruit outside the country.

The BIP sub-group was introduced by the Labour Government with the aim of attracting self-employed business migrants with capital to invest in New Zealand. The naivety of this first scheme was reflected in the low level of capital required, set at $100,000, the average price of a house. This amount is hardly substantial enough to set up manufacturing businesses likely to provide employment. There was also no monitoring to ensure that businesses were established or that the money was not remitted back to the home country to allow another migrant to use it as a ticket of entry. Indeed, anecdotal evidence suggests that this was the case.

The report noted there were four significant changes in immigration policy in recent years. There was a doubling of immigration applicants from 10,000 to 20,500 between 1986 and 1990. There were increases in the social category to 153 percent, the economic category to 89 percent and the humanitarian category to 31 percent. There was also an increase in overstayers from 13,000 in 1986 to 20,000 in 1990.[28] A radical change in the source of immigrants was also noted. Immigrants from the United Kingdom fell from 36 percent in 1986 to 16 percent in 1990. On the other hand, Hong Kong, Taiwan and Malaysia have become major countries of origin.[29]

The report does not question why immigration from Asia has increased. The imminent hand-over of Hong Kong to mainland China is one obvious explanation; overcrowding, pollution and repressive governments are other possible reasons for immigrants abandoning their own countries. In other words, the motives of immigrants are more likely to be egocentric rather than a sense of migrating to make a contribution to the commonweal of New Zealand.

The points system

The working party recommended the introduction of a points system in an attempt to control the number and quality of immigrants into New Zealand. A scale of 1–10 points was allocated to two out of four sub-sections for the category of employability, namely education/qualifications, business/work experience, special skills including entrepreneurial, and offers of skilled employment. A candidate could score a maximum of twenty points for employability. The age factor of immigrants was also assessed on ten points, with the maximum going to immigrants between twenty-five and twenty-nine years of age. In the financial independence category, $100,000 for settlement and purchase of a house gained five points, and one point could be gained for each additional $100,000 to be remitted. This category had a maximum of ten points. Other settlement factors include language skills (one to four points), and one point for a New Zealand sponsor, relative in the country, and a local authority or group sponsor.[30]

The working party recommended that business immigrants be placed in a category of their own, with fast-track procedures guaranteeing residence, to encourage them to use this route of entry ahead of other categories for which they might well qualify. The ideal, the working party suggests, is business immigrants with capital in excess of $500,000, whereby the hoped for benefit to the economy is likely to be realised.[31] This is the first intimation that perhaps the earlier BIP scheme of the previous government had not done what it was supposed to do.

Proposals to tighten up vetting and monitoring procedures include the interview of candidates by a panel of three persons, two in business and one from the Immigration Service; and lodgement of funds in a trust account to be disbursed for investment in projects approved by the panel. This latter proposal would effectively close the loophole of the same funds being remitted back and forth to bring out successive immigrants.

To implement a proactive immigration policy, the

working party recommend the establishment of a marketing section in the Immigration Section to promote New Zealand as a destination for quality migrants.

The Asian invasion

Statistics supplied by the Immigration Service lists ninety-seven countries as the source of immigrants coming into New Zealand. But the numbers are not evenly distributed. A total of 21,927 immigrants entered the country in 1990. Of that number, 11,219 came from Asian countries such as Malaysia, Taiwan, Singapore, Korea, Hong Kong et al. On the other hand, immigrants from our own region in the South Pacific were down by 50 percent, from 10,227 in 1989 to 4,320 in 1990. This alteration in our immigration pattern is dollar driven by the Government's BIP and 'skilled immigrants' policy. Asian capital is wanted ahead of Pacific Island labour.

Businesses established by Asians on the amount of capital designated by the BIP scheme will have certain characteristics. First, they are likely to be small enterprises with few employees. Secondly, they will probably be launched on family labour or personnel from the same ethnic stock as the entrepreneur to minimise start-up costs. Thirdly, such businesses will have a low-wage structure. Some are likely to pay wages in cash, so there will be no record of taxable income on immigrant workers. Yet immigrants, on gaining residency, become immediately eligible for the host country's education, health and social benefits.

At the outset, the Government should have kept records of who came in under the BIP scheme, and run spot-checks to see what businesses they started, and how many New Zealanders they employed. Only when accurate data can be provided by the Government through stringent research can the worth of the scheme be proved and its continuation countenanced. Without that data, the validity of the BIP scheme has yet to be proved.

As it is, the BIP is being promoted by the Minister of Immigration like a monk uttering a mantra. If it is repeated often enough it will bring about an economic miracle. There is no place for religion in politics. Politics is about reality, not what might be.

The nearest thing to a justification of the BIP scheme comes from Dr Manying Ip, of Auckland University, who said the 'Asian Invasion' should be welcomed so as to capitalise on the wealth and success of Asian migrants.[32] Dr Ip cited data from the Commerce Ministry indicating that Chinese migrants moved $800 million into New Zealand during 1988 and 1989. Over 200 businesses were established, 770 jobs created and $13.4 million paid in wages. Impressive as these data are, they are qualitatively deficient. They do not tell us whether they are manufacturing or service businesses, and how many New Zealanders were among those employed. Assuming that Asian immigrants with an annual inflow of 11,000 plus will take up some of those jobs, the number of jobs created is insufficient for their own needs let alone those of the rising number of unemployed New Zealanders.

The beneficiaries

If there is no evidence yet of unemployed New Zealanders benefiting from the Government's immigration policy, who are the beneficiaries of the scheme? The most obvious, of course, are the immigrants themselves. They have escaped from overcrowded, traffic-congested, pollution-plagued homelands, often with repressive governments, to a land which is idyllic in comparison. The good fortune is theirs, and they are not begrudged that. But, should we continue the policy being followed now and double our population every thirty years, it is only a matter of time before the conditions from which the immigrants have escaped will be replicated here.

The growing inflow of Asian immigrants creates some employment for immigrants who arrived in the first wave. They act as mediators in the settlement of later immigrants into the host society. Trevor Mok, a Chinese from Malaysia, for instance, is doing well selling real estate to business immigrants settling in Wellington.[33] In August, the Auckland Savings Bank appointed Anthony Wang manager of the bank's new Immigration and Financial Advisory Division. New employment was also created for Asians in twelve suburban branches of the ASB. Migrants from the Pacific were never given this kind of consideration by the banks.

There are other beneficiaries of the BIP scheme, but they are less obvious. They are the immigrant consultants who, through private practice, have increasingly taken over from the Immigration Service the function of processing immigrant papers and facilitating entry into New Zealand for a fee. The fees are lucrative. They range from $2,000 up to $100,000. Typically, a business migrant employing a consultant would agree to a fee of $10,000.[34]

There is a varied group of organisations involved in immigration consultancy. Accounting and legal firms process immigrants' papers as an adjunct to their main activities. But since the inception of the BIP scheme in 1987, private individuals have set themselves up as immigration consultants. Some of the high-profile consultants are former politicians with inside knowledge of the operation of government bureaucracies and immigration laws. One of the better known is Malcolm Consultants Ltd, whose principal is the Hon. A. G. Malcolm, a former Minister of Immigration. He has offices in London, West Germany, Taiwan and Hong Kong.[35] Malcolm's advertisement in the *New Zealand/Taiwan Trade and Investment Year Book* states:

> For any individual wishing to gain permanent residence in New Zealand, the most difficult part of all is to be accepted as a Malcolm Consultants' client. On becoming a client, however, success is guaranteed . . . a great strength of the company is a close working knowledge of New Zealand Government procedures and New Zealand Government personnel.

Sir Roger Douglas, also a Minister of Immigration from 1989–90, recently joined the ranks of consultants with Dunlop Kidd Ltd, a consultancy targeting business immigrants. Dr Michael Bassett, a former Minister of Internal

Affairs, set up his own business and occupational consultancy when he retired from politics in 1990. He has since been recruited by Dunlop Kidd as well.[36] The business of immigration consultancy has grown so rapidly in the last two years that Malcolm Consultants formed the New Zealand Association of Immigration Consultants in July 1991.

Employers are also beneficiaries of the occupational category of the Government's immigration policy whereby they can recruit off-shore personnel if they can demonstrate there are no suitable candidates in New Zealand. Although the numbers are small, employers and immigration consultants have been known to collude in tailoring job descriptions to eliminate local candidates and recruit overseas personnel. Some of the job descriptions are so prescriptive, in citing foreign language skills that do not appear to be necessary for the job, that it is impossible for New Zealanders to apply.[37]

Overseas experience

Immigrants from non-European countries require housing, education, hospitals, health care, ESL schools and capital investment to create jobs. In Australia, the cost is $80,000 per head.[38] The total cost to Australia of settling multicultural immigrants is almost $8 billion – a cost added to the deficit in the balance of payments.[39]

A study by the Australian Department of Immigration and Ethnic Affairs concluded that immigration as a tool for short-term management was not suitable. The macroeconomic consequences were negligible.[40] Added to the economic cost was the social cost of lack of public accountability in immigration procedures, maladministration and inadequate screening of immigrants with criminal backgrounds.

Dr Baker, Chairman of the Australian Academy of Science, and Dr Flannery cite environmental degradation as a negative feature of population growth due to immigration. In overcrowded countries, people resort to destroying the environment in order to survive. The competition for food is so intense that there is no ethic of conservation. In the host country, immigrants with their own ethnic culture take limpets, sea-urchins, undersize fish, indeed anything with flesh to eat from hundreds of inter-tidal areas and rock pools.[41]

In view of the mounting evidence against immigration as a method of stimulating economic growth, Australia has rejected it as a solution. The head of the Australian Economic Planning Advisory Council concluded that the capital demand on the host country exceeds the gains, so he recommended scrapping the BIP scheme.

Immigration, particularly the illegal immigration of refugees, is of vital concern in overcrowded European countries. They are tightening up entry procedures. France, for instance, rejected 100,000 foreigners and Italy 30,000. Switzerland is concerned about thousands of illegal refugees who have entered the country from Yugoslavia and the Middle East.[42]

In East Germany there were 85,000 *gastarbeiter* (guest-workers) from Vietnam, Angola, and Mozambique. They did the communal dirty work as unskilled labourers and in construction jobs. But with the unification of Germany, unemployment has risen in the Eastern sector. Associated with rising unemployment is an outbreak of xenophobia and racism. The guest workers are being thrown out and told to 'go home' before things get nasty.[43]

The losers of proactive immigration

In the nineteenth century, Māori leaders welcomed immigrants from Europe for trade and the economic benefits they brought to New Zealand. In the first two decades after the Treaty of Waitangi, the hoped-for prosperity was realised as tribes planted wheat, processed it with their own flour mills and transported the flour and other produce from the land in their own coastal vessels to the markets.[44] But after 1858, when the immigrants achieved numerical superiority and political dominance, the hegemony of the nation state

over the indigenous population was asserted by violence.
Māori land and resources were expropriated through the
judicial apparatus of the state and the Māori consigned to
the underclass status of the brown proletariat.

Although the consequences of the present immigration
policy might not be as disastrous for the nation as it was for
the Māori, nevertheless some of the negative outcomes of
immigration in other countries are already being replicated
here. They impinge on both Māori and Pākehā.

While advocating business immigration on one hand,
Mr Birch, the Minister of Immigration, is aiming to expel
from New Zealand our own guest-workers from the South
Pacific. Now that their labour is no longer needed by the
political economy, 7,467 Samoans, 4,920 Tongans, and 1,035
Fijians classed as overstayers are wanted out.[45] In the
meantime, illegal immigrants and foreign workers from
China, India and elsewhere are being exploited by the
kiwifruit farmers in the Bay of Plenty, the orchardists of
Nelson and on industrial sites of our cities.

Kiwifruit contractors in the Bay of Plenty claim there
are 200 illegal immigrants, mainly Indians, working in the
Katikati-Ōmokoroa area for as little as $2 an hour. The
contractors resent their livelihood being undermined and
want the immigrants out.[46] Similarly, the New Zealand
Workers' Union has declared its opposition to illegal foreign
workers picking fruit in Nelson without work permits.[47]
Some Chinese on visitor's permits were reputedly working
on building sites in Auckland for as little as $2 or $3 an hour.
Unionists in the building trade resent these immigrant
workers knocking down conditions that took them 150 years
to achieve.[48] In Auckland, four Chinese cooks brought out
from Hong Kong in 1989 to work in the Orient Towers
Restaurant arrived to find the building incomplete. They
were employed illegally on the site as electrical labourers
and as cooks in their employer's house in the evening. They
were left destitute when dismissed by their employer.[49]

The Australian experience of wholesale harvesting of
marine life by immigrants is also being replicated in New
Zealand. A newspaper headline 'Shellfish being stripped by

immigrants unaware of law'[50] sounded an early warning of the environmental impact of bringing people into New Zealand who do not have an ethic of conservation. The Royal Forest and Bird Protection Society is concerned over people 'strip-mining' rockpools at Muriwai of marine creatures.[51] Sea-eggs, starfish and chitons are taken by the sackful, as well as mussels and other species.

An even more serious threat to marine resources is posed by entrepreneurs exporting undersized and illegally taken pāua to Asia. Two Asian company directors, along with four others, appeared in the Auckland District Court in July 1990 charged with 255 offences against the Fisheries Act.[52] We need to remind ourselves and the Government that the people we are inviting to share our country are the very people who introduced drift-net fishing to the world. The same people continue to hunt whales against mounting world opinion calling for a ban on whaling.

In 1987, the Government allowed citizens from Malaysia, Singapore, Indonesia and Thailand to enter New Zealand without visas. This policy of easy access has opened New Zealand to criminals from overseas and to unethical practices by visitors wanting to gain permanent residency. Headlines proclaiming New Zealand a 'Target of big racket in passports',[53] 'Marriage scams and welfare fraud linked',[54] 'Thai woman tells of prostitution trap'[55] and 'Police bust immigrant crime ring'[56] indicate the Government's naivety in opening up the country to the rest of the world at a time when the nations of Europe are trying to insulate their borders against outsiders.

It is futile for Mr Birch to warn immigration consultants to ensure that business migrants bring in 'clean money'[57] when neither they, nor the Government, have the capacity to investigate the bona fides of a business immigrant. The consultant's sole interest is in the fee for getting their client into the country. As far as they are concerned, they have discharged their responsibility for character screening if the client signs the statutory declaration that they have not been convicted of criminal activity or are not wanted in their own country.

Harvey Misbin, the most celebrated business immigrant in this category, established the freight carrier Southern World Airlines New Zealand. A *Frontline* television documentary programme reported that Misbin, who was granted New Zealand residency and later citizenship, was wanted in the United States for alleged smuggling of cocaine from South America to the United States.[58]

Another high-flying entrepreneur, Ralf Simon, who planned to buy the Pakatoa island resort, is wanted in Germany on criminal charges.[59] Official investigation of business immigrants who make false declarations about their criminal past become a charge on the New Zealand taxpayer.

The last word on BIP comes from the immigrants themselves. Some say it is too difficult to make money in New Zealand's depressed economy let alone create jobs. Business returns have been so low that some businessmen were looking to return to Taiwan and Hong Kong. The Executive Director of the Hwa Hsia Society for Taiwan migrants, Karl Chen, said it was very hard to set up industrial plants or other business here. The local market was small, labour costs high, unions too strong, New Zealand too far away from material suppliers, and sea freight costs were high.[60]

In view of these admissions, together with mounting evidence of negative outcomes from immigration on the quality of life in New Zealand, the Business Immigration Policy of the Government should be suspended pending a public inquiry into its viability.

30 September 1991
(Seminar, Māori Studies Department, University of Auckland)

Looking to Asia

URING THE winter months, the managers of the political economy launched the Asia 2000 promotion. Leading the charge was the Prime Minister, Jim Bolger, who proclaimed New Zealand to be an Asian country. This redefinition of who we are as a people was reinforced by the Minister of Immigration, Mr McKinnon, who said New Zealand's future lies with Asia. The Minister of Education, Dr Lockwood Smith, also chimed in with a call to teach Mandarin Chinese in our schools.

I was flabbergasted to put it mildly. For as long as I can remember, we thought of ourselves as a European country, until Mother England unkindly cut us adrift when she joined the European Common Market in the seventies. Gradually, our sense of who we are, and our place in the world, came to focus on the Pacific. Closer Economic Relations with Australia, together with the South Pacific Forum of prime ministers, helped to define our identity as a Pacific nation. In fact we felt secure enough in that identity to turn our back on a surrogate mother in the United States by closing our ports to nuclear-armed and propelled vessels. In a show of sovereign independence, we enshrined that decision in legislation.

But showing some spine on the world stage was short-lived as the stagnant economy refused to respond immediately to its restructuring by Rogernomics in the eighties. Corporatisation of bureaucracies, the sale of state assets, the free market, and the depowering of unions have served only to enrich the few while heaping misery on the unemployed. Desperate for a quick fix, our leaders cranked up a Business Immigration Policy and opened the door to 'skilled' immigrants from Asia and the rest of the world. The rationale is that these entrepreneurial migrants will create jobs for New Zealanders. Now, without asking us, the politicians have made us an appendage of Asia, because they perceive it to be the economic powerhouse of the future.

Two changes of identity in two decades is more than I

can handle. I liked us being a Pacific nation, and resent being told by our Prime Minister we are an Asian nation. The reason for this schizophrenic behaviour is trade. The Minister of Trade, Phillip Burdon, chided New Zealanders for xenophobic attitudes towards Asia, a region which now takes 30 percent of our exports. Of particular interest is China, the waking giant with a staggering growth rate of 13 percent. The managers of the political economy, namely Cabinet and the Business Roundtable, want a piece of that action. Rightly so. But surely we don't have to turn belly up and become an Asian nation in order to win trade by opening our borders up to migrants from over ninety-seven countries?

There are 100 million economic refugees around the world looking for a better life. We are only one of five nations, including our Australian, Canadian and American cousins, who are willing to take some of them in. But that will change. There is a growing awareness that the post-modern ideology of multiculturalism has a corrosive effect on the nation state and its sense of national identity. Para-doxically, leading the debate is the United States. But then we shouldn't be too surprised as the multicultural experi-ment in California has resulted in social breakdown, ethnic violence and white flight. In the last year, half a million people left California. Not far behind in growing opposition to immigration and multiculturalism is Australia.

The discourse in New Zealand has hardly begun. But there is growing awareness at the base level of xenophobia, immigrants taking jobs, and racism. Only the journalist Pat Booth, with his 'Asian Invasion' article in the *Eastern Courier*, dared to write about it. For the liberals and intelligentsia, it is too sensitive an issue. They know that the pro-immigration lobby will lumber anyone who opposes the Roundtable's thrust towards Asia, and the Government's immigration policy supporting it, with the label of racism.

Leading the debate in the United States is the Foundation for Immigration Reform (FAIR). FAIR was founded fifteen years ago by Dr John Tanton, an intellectual and humanist. At first, Tanton set aside one day of the week to work on ecological and environmental concerns. Eventually he realised his efforts would come to nought if America continued to take in over a million legal and illegal immigrants a year. He concluded that filling America with people would, in the long-term, bring about environmental degradation. Tanton turned his energy towards immigration reform.

FAIR based its charter for reform on this statement from the 1972 Rockefeller Commission of Inquiry on Population Growth and the American Future:

> We have concluded that . . . no substantive benefits will result from further growth of the nation's population . . . We have looked for, and not found, any convincing economic argument for continued population growth. The health of our country does not depend on it, nor does the vitality of business nor the welfare of the average person.

The members of FAIR are the intelligentsia, the academic and professional class of middle America. It is a respectable organisation whose advice is increasingly sought by Senators and Congressmen on the vexed questions of immigration. For FAIR, the payoff is in sight with the tabling in the Senate of an Omnibus Bill on Immigration by Senator Reid of Nevada. The bill, designed by FAIR, aims to curb criminal activity by aliens, protect American workers from unfair labour competition, relieve charges on welfare and public services by strengthening border security to stop illegal immigration, and cut legal immigration down by two-thirds.

America is leading on immigration reform. Australia is trailing, while New Zealand is not yet in the race.

26 October 1993
(*Metro*)

References

In the beginning

1 D. Simmons, *Whakairo*, p. 17.
2 Sir Peter Buck, *The Coming of the Maori*, p. 434.
3 Sir Peter Buck, loc. cit.
4 Sir George Grey, *Nga Mahi a Nga Tupuna*, p. 1.
5 Sir George Grey, loc. cit.
6 Sir Peter Buck, op. cit., p. 435.
7 Sir George Grey, op. cit., p. 17.
8 Sir George Grey, op. cit., p. 2.
9 Sir George Grey, op. cit., p. 4.
10 Sir Peter Buck, op. cit., pp. 450–52.
11 J. McEwen, *Rangitane*, p. 5.
12 P. T. H. Jones, *King Potatau*, p. 264.

Taha Māori

1 J. E. Ritchie, *The Making of a Maori*, p. 39.
2 J. Metge, *A New Maori Migration*, p. 94.
3 K. Sinclair, *A History of New Zealand*, p. 14.
4 Sir P. H. Buck, *The Coming of the Maori*, p. 37.
5 D. Simmons, *Settlement of the Maori in New Zealand*, p. 207.

6 R. Green, *A Review of the Prehistoric Sequence in the Auckland Province*, p. 14.
7 D. Simmons, *Settlement of the Maori in New Zealand*, p. 205.
8 D. Simmons, *The Great New Zealand Myth*, p. 32.
9 J. Metge, *A New Maori Migration*, pp. 124–24.
10 R. Firth, *Economics of the New Zealand Maori*, p. 390.
11 D. Simmons, *The Great New Zealand Myth*, p. 321.

The genesis of the meeting house as a cultural symbol

1 Green 1970, p. 12.
2 Davidson 1984, p. 40.
3 Davidson 1984, p. 116.
4 Simmons 1975, p. 207.
5 Green 1970, p. 14.
6 Simmons 1975, p. 205.
7 Davidson 1984, p. 184.
8 Groube 1964, p. 84.
9 Beaglehole 1963, pp. 17–18.
10 Groube 1964, p. 10.
11 Grey 1953, pp. 1–198.
12 Te Wānanga Vol 1, No 2 pp. 141–260; Vol 11, No 1, pp. 121–180.
13 Pōhuhu 1930, p. 150.
14 Pōhuhu 1930, p. 153.
15 Grey 1953, p. 12.
16 Grey 1953, p. 16.

17 Grey 1953, pp. 29–30.
18 Grey 1953, pp. 32–35.
19 Grey 1953, p. 52.
20 Grey 1953, pp. 29–30.
21 Best 1952, p. 241.
22 Buck 1950, pp. 113–36.
23 Pricket 1982, p. 119.
24 Pricket 1979, p. 43.
25 Sutton, p. 541.
26 Davidson, p. 153.
27 Davidson, p. 153.
28 Simmons, pp. 13–14.
29 McEwen, p. 408.
30 McEwen, p. 409.
31 Simmons, p. 13.
32 Mead, p. 35.
33 Groube, pp. 85–89.
34 Groube, p. 120.
35 Murray-Oliver, p. 47.
36 Groube, p. 118.
37 Biggs and Mead, p. 35.
38 Kelly, p. 35.
39 Kelly, pp. 71–72.
40 Cruise, p. 115.
41 Polack, p. 31.
42 Salmond, p. 80.
43 Sinclair, p. 83.
44 Sinclair, p. 85.
45 Simmons, pp. 28–37.
46 Phillips, p. 20.
47 Barrow, p. 40.
48 Phillips, p. ii.
49 Barrow, p. 78.
50 Barrow, pp. 33–35.
51 Barrow, p. 11.
52 Phillips, pp. 7–11.
53 Fowler, p. 2.
54 Barrow, p. 84.
55 Simmons, p. 121.
56 King, p. 183.
57 King, p. 136.
58 King, p. 142.
59 Ramsden, pp. 45–46.

The Treaty of Waitangi as the focus of Māori protest

1 Government Printer, *Introduction to Facsimiles of the Treaty of Waitangi*.
2 A. F. McDonnell, *Te Manukura*, p. 10.
3 R. Ross, 'The Treaty on the ground', in *The Treaty of Waitangi, Its Origins and Significance*, p. 16.
4 P. Adams, *Fatal Necessity*, p. 235.
5 W. Colenso, *The Authentic and Genuine History of the Signing of the Treaty of Waitangi*, p. 20.
6 T. L. Buick, *The Treaty of Waitangi*, p. 128.
7 T. L. Buick, op. cit., p. 137.
8 T. L. Buick, op. cit., p. 142.
9 T. L. Buick, op. cit., p. 59.
10 T. L. Buick, op. cit., p. 218.
11 G. W. Rusden, *Auretanga*, p. 6.
12 H. Evison, *Ngai Tahu Land Rights*, pp. 32–33.
13 H. Miller, *Race Conflict in New Zealand*, p. 30.
14 G. W. Rusden, *Auretanga*, pp. 22–23.
15 A. Ward, *A Show of Justice*, p. 272.
16 G. W. Rusden, *Auretanga*, p. 162.
17 Māori Parliament, 1892, pp. 1–26.

18 M. King, *Te Puea*, p. 75.

Tradition and change in Māori leadership

1   R. Firth, *Economics of the New Zealand Maori*, pp. 111–115.
2   R. Firth, op. cit., p. 114.
3   R. Firth, op. cit., p. 114.
4   K. Sinclair, *A History of New Zealand*, p. 35.
5   B. Elsemore, *Like Them That Dream*, p. 14.
6   K. Sinclair, op. cit., p. 43.
7   R. Ruth, *The Treaty of Waitangi: Its Origins and Significance*, p. 27.
8   A. Gramsci, *Selections from Prison Notebooks*, p. 12.
9   H. Evison, *Ngai Tahu Land Rights*, pp. 17–32.
10 P. Te Hurinui, *King Potatau*, p. 223.
11 R. Walker, *Struggle Without End*, p. 168.
12 H. Riseborough, *Days of Darkness*, pp. 168–71.
13 R. Walker, op. cit. p. 168.
14 A. Gramsci, *Selections from Prison Notebooks*, p. 3.
15 P. Freire, *Pedagogy of the Oppressed*, pp. 126–27.
16 A. Gramsci, op. cit., p. 12.
17 Sir Apirana Ngata, *The Treaty of Waitangi*, p. 5.
18 G. Butterworth, *Sir Apirana Ngata*, pp. 26–27.
19 R. Walker, op. cit., p. 195.
20 J. K. Hunn, *Report on the Department of Maori Affairs*, p. 9.
21 Whakakotahi Task Force Discussion Paper No. 7, p. 4.

Direct negotiation and the fiscal envelope

1   Michel Foucault, *Power/ Knowledge*, pp. 104–105.
2   R. J. Walker, *Struggle Without End*, p. 255.
3   R. J. Walker, op. cit., p. 265.
4   David Held, *Introduction to Critical Theory*, p. 7.
5   Her Majesty the Queen and Maori Deed of Settlement, p. 16.
6   Loc. cit., p. 22.

Education and power

1   A. Gramsci, *Selections from Prison Notebooks*, p. 12.
2   B. Elsmore, *Like Them That Dream*, p. 25.
3   J. Ewing and J. Shallcrass (eds), *Introduction to Maori Education*, p. 28.
4   R. J. Walker, *Struggle Without End*, p. 146.
5   R. J. Walker, op. cit., p. 195.
6   *AJHR*, 1906, G-5, p. 94.
7   *AJHR*, 1906, G-5, p. 96.
8   Simon, *The Place of Schooling in Māori-Pākehā Relations*, PhD thesis, University of Auckland, 1990, pp. 97–99.
9   *AJHR*, 1941, E-3, p. 3.
10 E. Schwimmer (ed.), *The Maori People in the Nineteen Sixties*, p. 74.

11 J. K. Hunn, *Report on the Department of Maori Affairs*, p. 25.

12 F. Riessman, *The Culturally Deprived Child*, pp. 1–47.

13 R. J. Walker, (ed.), Māori Educational Development Conference Report, University of Auckland, 1984, p. 27.

14 J. Codd, R. Harker, R. Nash (eds), *Political Issues in New Zealand Education*, p. 76.

15 R. Benton, *Who Speaks Māori in New Zealand?*, pp. 23–34.

16 D. Hughes, 'The Examination System', in *New Zealand Counselling and Guidance Journal*, 1983, p. 30.

17 R. J. Walker, op. cit., p. 194.

18 R. J. Walker (ed.), Maori Educational Development Conference Report, 1984, pp. 47–49.

The Government's economic mantra of BIP immigration

1 Ruth Ross, *The Treaty on the Ground*, p. 27.

2 Claudia Orange, *The Treaty of Waitangi*, p. 41.

3 Finding of the Waitangi Tribunal on the Manukau Claim, 1985, p. 91.

4 Muriwhenua Fishing Report, Waitangi Tribunal, 1988, pp. 307–14.

5 Facsimiles of the Treaty of Waitangi, 1976, p. 6.

6 Human Rights Commission Report to the Prime Minister on Migrant Workers, 1990, p. 19.

7 Hon. Tirikatene-Sullivan, Question No. 85, Office of the Clerk of the House of Representatives, 3 September 1991.

8 Review of Immigration Policy, 1986, p. 9.

9 Loc. cit.

10 Op. cit., p. 10.

11 Op. cit., p. 14–19.

12 Loc. cit.

13 J. Poot, G. Nana, B. Philpott, 1988, p. 150.

14 *People's Voice*, 2 September 1990, p. 22.

15 Wolfgang Kaspar, *Populate or Languish*, p. 42.

16 Op. cit., p. 47.

17 Op. cit., p. 12.

18 Op. cit., p. 45.

19 Paulo Freire, *Pedagogy of the Oppressed*, p. 31.

20 Op. cit., p. 36.

21 Kaspar, op. cit., p. 42.

22 Op. cit., pp. xiii–xiv.

23 Op. cit., p. 66.

24 Op. cit., p. 6.

25 Op. cit., p. 60.

26 Op. cit., p. 49.

27 Report of the Working Party on Immigration, 1991, p. 1.

28 Op. cit., pp. 1–5.

29 Loc. cit.

30 Op. cit., p. 10.

31 Op. cit., p. 18.

32 *Auckland Star*, 6 June 1990.

33 *New Zealand Listener*, 16 September 1991.

34 Op. cit., p. 21.
35 Report to the Prime Minister on Migrant Workers, 1990, p. 16, Human Rights Commission.
36 *New Zealand Herald*, 4 June 1991.
37 *Auckland Star*, 28 July 1991.
38 *The Bulletin*, 27 February 1990.
39 Op. cit., 28 May 1991.
40 Op. cit., 27 February 1990.
41 *The Dominion*, 3 July 1990.
42 *New Zealand Herald*, 9 September 1991.
43 *Harvard Business Review*, March-April 1991.
44 R. Walker, *Ka Whawhai Tonu Mātou*, pp. 99–101.
45 Hon. Bill Birch (Minister of Pacific Island Affairs, newsletter), June 1991.
46 *Sunday Star*, 30 June 1991.
47 *Nelson Evening Mail*, 21 January 1989.
48 *New Zealand Herald*, 16 October 1990.
49 *New Zealand Herald*, 30 June 1991.
50 *New Zealand Herald*, 10 January 1991.
51 *New Zealand Herald*, 15 June 1991.
52 *New Zealand Herald*, 18 July 1991.
53 *New Zealand Herald*, 12 November 1990.
54 *New Zealand Herald*, 29 May 1991.
55 *New Zealand Herald*, 25 September 1991.
56 *New Zealand Herald*, 21 September 1991.
57 *New Zealand Herald*, 29 July 1991.
58 *Sunday Star*, 29 September 1991.
59 *Sunday Star*, 6 October 1991.
60 *New Zealand Herald*, 26 September 1991.

Bibliography

Adams, P., 1977, *Fatal Necessity*, Auckland University Press.

Barrow, T., 1969, *Maori Wood Sculpture*, A. H. & A. W. Reed. Wellington.

Beaglehole, J. C., (ed.), 1962, *The Endeavour Journal of Joseph Banks*, Vol. II, Angus and Robertson, Sydney.

Benton, R., 1979, *Who Speaks Maori in New Zealand?*, New Zealand Council for Educational Research, Wellington.

Best, E., 1952, *The Maori As He Was*, Government Printer, Wellington.

Biggs, B., & Mead, S. M., (eds), 1964. *He Kohikohinga Aronui*, Anthropology Department, University of Auckland.

Buck, Sir Peter, 1950, *The Coming of the Maori*, Maori Purposes Fund Board, Whitcombe & Tombs, Wellington.

Buick, T. L., 1936, *The Treaty of Waitangi*, Thomas Avery & Sons, New Plymouth, Capper Press Reprint 1976, Christchurch.

Butterworth, G., 1968, *Sir Apirana Ngata*, A. H. & A. W. Reed, Wellington.

Codd, J., Harker, R., Nash, R., (eds), 1985, *Political Issues in New Zealand Education*, Dunmore Press, Palmerston North.

Colenso, W., 1890, *The Authentic and Genuine History of the Signing of the Treaty of Waitangi*, Capper Reprint, 1971.

Cruise, R. A., 1824, *Journal of Ten Months' Residence in New Zealand*, Longman Hurst and Co., London.

Davidson, J., 1984, *The Prehistory of New Zealand*, Longman Paul, Auckland.

Elsmore, B., 1985, *Like Them That Dream*, Tauranga Moana Press.

Evison, H. C., 1987, *Ngai Tahu Land Rights*, Ngai Tahu Maori Trust Board, Christchurch.

Ewing, J., & Shallcrass, J., (eds), 1970, *Introduction To Maori Education*, New Zealand University Press, Price Milburn, Wellington.

Facsimilies of the Treaty of Waitangi, Government Printer, Wellington.

Firth, R., 1959, *Economics of the New Zealand Maori*, Whitcombe & Tombs, Wellington.

Foucault, M., 1980, *Power/Knowledge*, Pantheon Books, New York.

Friere, P., 1972, *Pedagogy of the Oppressed*, Penguin Books, Harmondsworth.

Fowler, L., 1974, *Te Mana o Turanga*, Penrose Printing and Publishing, Auckland.

Gramsci, A., 1982, *Selections from Prison Notebooks*, Lawrence & Wishart, London.

Green, R., 1970, *A Review of the Prehistoric Sequence in the Auckland Province*, University Bookshop, Dunedin.

Grey, Sir George, 1953, *Nga Mahi a Nga Tupuna*, Maori Purposes Fund Board, Wellington.

——, 1956, *Polynesian Mythology*, Whitcombe & Tombs Ltd., Wellington.

Groube, L., 1964, 'Settlement Patterns in Prehistoric New Zealand', MA thesis, University of Auckland.

Held, D., 1980, *Introduction To Critical Theory*, University of California Press, Berkeley.

Horton, P. B., & Hunt, C. L., 1972, *Sociology*, McGraw-Hill Kogashu, Tokyo.

Hughes, D., 1983. 'The Examination System: The Cause of Unnecessary Failure', *New Zealand Counselling and Guidance Journal*, Vol. 5, No. 1.

Hunn, J. K., 1960, *Report on the Department of Maori Affairs*, Government Printer, Wellington.

Jones, P. T. H., 1959, *King Potatau*, Polynesian Society, Wellington.

Kaspar, W., 1990, *Populate or Languish*, Wellington.

Kelly, L. G., 1949, *Tainui*, Polynesian Society, Wellington.

King, M., 1977, *Te Puea*, Hodder & Stoughton, Auckland.

Manning. F. E., 1973, *Old New Zealand*, Golden Press in association with Whitcombe & Tombs, Auckland.

McDonell, A. F., 1916, *Te Manukura*, The Maori Recorder, Vol. I, No. 1, Auckland.

McEwen, J. M., 1966, 'Maori Art', in McKlintock, A. H. (ed.), *Encyclopedia of New Zealand*, Government Printer, Wellington.

——, 1986, *Rangitane, A Tribal History*, Reed Methuen, Auckland.

Mead, S. M., (ed.), 1984, *Te Maori*, Heinemann, Auckland.

Metge, Joan, 1964, *A New Maori Migration*, University of London, Athlone Press.

Miller, H., 1966, *Race Conflict in New Zealand*, Blackwood & Janet Paul, Auckland.

Ngā Pepa a Ranginui

Murray-Oliver, A., 1968, *Augustus Earle in New Zealand*, Whitcombe
& Tombs, Christchurch.

Ngata, Sir A. T., 1922, *The Treaty of Waitangi*, Maori Purposes Fund
Board, Wellington.

Orange, C., 1987, *The Treaty of Waitangi*, Allen & Unwin, in
association with the Port Nicholson Press, Wellington.

Phillips, W. J., *Carved Maori Houses of Western and Northern Areas of
New Zealand*, Dominion Museum Monograph No. 9,
Government Printer, Wellington.

Pohuhu, N., 1930, Memoir Supplement, in *Te Wananga*, Vol. 1, No. 2,
Maori Purposes Fund Board, Wellington.

Polack, J., 1839, *New Zealand*, Vol. 1, Capper Reprint.

Poot, J., Nana, G., Philpott, B., *International Migration and the New
Zealand Economy*, Institute of Policy Studies, Victoria University
Press, Wellington.

Pricket, N., 1979, 'Prehistoric Occupation in the Moikau Valley,
Palliser Bay', in *Prehistoric Man in Palliser Bay*, edited by B. F.
Leach and H. M. Leach, National Museum of New Zealand,
Bulletin 21.

——, 1982, 'An Archaeologist's Guide to the Maori Dwelling',
NZJA.

Ramsden, E., 1948, *Sir Apirana Ngata*, Reed, Wellington.

Riessman, F., 1962, *The Culturally Deprived Child*, Harper & Row,
New York.

Riseborough, H., 1989, *Days of Darkness*, Allen & Unwin, Port
Nicholson Press, Wellington.

Ritchie, J., 1963, *The Making of a Maori*, A. H. & A. W. Reed,
Wellington.

Rusden, G. W., 1974, *Aureretanga*, Hakaprint, Cannon's Creek.

Salmond, A., 1975, *Hui*, A. H. & A. W. Reed, Wellington.

Schwimmer, E., 1968, *Maori People in the Nineteen Sixties*, Blackwood
& Janet Paul, Auckland.

Simmons, D. R., 1975, 'Settlement of the Maoris in New Zealand', in
The New Zealanders, Siers, J., & Henderson, J., Millwood Press,
Wellington.

——, 1976, *The Great New Zealand Myth*, A. H. & A. W. Reed,
Wellington.

——, 1985, *Whakairo*, Oxford University Press, Auckland.

Simon, J., 1990, 'The Place of Schooling in Māori Pakeha Relations',
PhD thesis, University of Auckland.

Sinclair, K., 1959, *A History of New Zealand*, Penguin Books, Harmondsworth.

Sutton, D., 1991, 'The Archaeology of Belief: Structuralism in Stratigraphical Context', in Pawley, A., (ed.), *Man and a Half*, Polynesian Society, Auckland.

Te Wananga, 1929, Vol. I, No. 2, Vol. II, No. 1, Maori Purposes Fund Board, Wellington.

The Treaty of Waitangi, Its Origins and Significance, 1972, Department of University Extension, Wellington.

Waitangi Tribunal Reports:

    1985, Finding of the Waitangi Tribunal on the Manukau Claim, Government Printer, Wellington.

    1988, Muriwhenua Fishing Report, Department of Justice, Government Printer, Wellington.

Ward, A., 1973, *A Show of Justice*, Auckland University Press.

Walker, R., (ed), 1984, *Nga Tumanako, Maori Educational Development Conference*, Report of the hui at Turangawaewae Marae, Centre for Continuing Education, University of Auckland.

——, 1990, *Ka Whawhai Tonu Mātou, Struggle Without End*, Penguin Books, Auckland.